# The CEO X factor

'KC's second book, *The CEO X factor*, is a sober reminder that we need to continue to tell our own stories – to describe, define and shape this landscape in our own image for the simple fact that no people can be helped by, nor benefit from, institutions that are not a direct result of their own character. [The book] offers a fantastic opportunity to drink from the pool of excellence and wallow in the presence of dignified greatness.

It is also a reminder of [British writer] George Monbiot's quote that "if wealth was the inevitable result of hard work and enterprise, every woman in Africa would be a millionaire".'

*– Bonang Mohale*, author, business leader and
president of Business Unity South Africa

'In a world where so many are crying out for mentorship, *The CEO X factor* certainly helps to fill the void. Get insight and access to valuable lessons learnt from those who have made it to the top from a South African business leadership perspective. If you are looking to climb the corporate ladder or you are simply wanting a glimpse of what it takes to run a business, *The CEO X factor* is a must-read.'

*– Bronwyn Nielsen*, former editor-in-chief of
CNBC Africa and founder of The Nielsen Network

# The CEO X factor

## Secrets for Success from South Africa's Top Money Makers

KC ROTTOK CHESAINA

Jonathan Ball Publishers
Johannesburg • Cape Town

Text © KC Rottok Chesaina (2023)
Cover image © Shameel Joosub – Courtesy of Vodacom, Ryan Noach – Courtesy of Discovery,
Mteto Nyati – Courtesy of Altron, Mpumi Madisa – Courtesy of Bidvest,
Leila Fourie – Devin Lester,  Edward Kieswetter – Mzu Nhlabati,
Polo Leteka – Bridget Corke Photography, Gerrie Fourie – Courtesy of Capitec.

Published edition © Jonathan Ball Publishers (2023)

Published in South Africa in 2023 by
JONATHAN BALL PUBLISHERS
A division of Media24 (Pty) Ltd
PO Box 33977
Jeppestown
2043

ISBN 978-1-77619-238-0
ebook ISBN 978-1-77619-239-7

www.jonathanball.co.za
www.twitter.com/JonathanBallPub
www.facebook.com/JonathanBallPublishers

Cover by Sean Robertson
Design and typesetting by Nazli Jacobs

For my progeny and future CEOs,
Yano and Jemator.

# Contents

# FOREWORD

Societal progress, whether it be in the arts, sports, politics, religion or the economy, has never manifested itself in a linear way. It is precisely because societal development doesn't follow a straight line from one point to the next that it matters how societal endeavours are organised and led.

In this regard, two important things should be considered: institutions – as in the structures through which societal endeavours are organised – and the people who lead them.

History has shown that the most effective and efficient way of organising economic activity is through corporates, making them the most dominant form. That's not to ignore the problems that come with how these corporate structures have been abused by the people entrusted to lead them. In South Africa, the private sector accounts for about 75% of the country's economic activity; the state the remainder.

I have been lucky in that I have over the years been involved in societal institutions in business, politics, the church and the trade union movement. Key to all of these societal endeavours, in my experience, has been how they are organised (the institutions) and the quality of leadership of those institutions.

In all the endeavours I have been involved in, including as Minister of Finance, I learnt the importance of leadership. It's not only about determining an agenda (what one would like to achieve), but also about mobilising the resources required to achieve that agenda. In politics, as I'm sure the case is in other fields, one must also mobilise support for one's agenda. Of course, by 'one's agenda' I don't only mean a personal one but a collective one.

As British historian Peter Clarke puts it, 'without an agenda [a "political programme" in South African parlance] and the mobilisation of support for it, nothing can get done in democratic politics. If leadership is partly a question of vision about the direction in which policy ought to be developed, it is also a matter of projecting electoral appeal and putting together a winning coalition of effective support,' he writes.[1]

Clarke adds that political leaders come in different forms – some are born great, others achieve greatness, and some have greatness thrust upon them. One can also say that one's given circumstances matter.

Clarke's point is that leaders differ – they are raised under different social and other circumstances. It's these different backgrounds – how, in the language of social scientists, each person is socialised – that explain the differences in their approach or their different leadership styles.

Given my own involvement in business, both in a family enterprise and the boards of companies I sit on, I was intrigued by how KC Rottok Chesaina would deal with corporate leadership, more specifically the special talent or quality – the X factor – of the CEOs he profiles in this book. It is those special qualities that help us understand how these individuals scaled the corporate heights, including starting businesses from scratch and building them into formidable economic institutions.

Again, place matters, because it often contains valuable clues to help explain how we became who we are. By place I mean not only the places where we are raised, but also the institutions we have presided over or worked at. American writer Robert A Caro says the places where we have been can shed light on our feelings, drives, motivations, self-confidence and insecurities.[2] By helping readers understand the forces that shaped a leader, a writer gives them perspective on the special talent or quality of that leader.

I believe after reading this book, readers will better understand the men and women profiled here. They will gain deeper insight into the places and other forces that have made them who they are today and, most importantly, help explain their achievements.

As I said at the beginning, leadership matters. It matters because it sets the tone of an institution. A leader who behaves like a pirate will drive the institution she or he leads into piracy. That's because any team takes their cue from its leader.

Particularly in politics, but also in other fields, much of leadership takes place in the glare of TV cameras and the media. It's often very public and this matters. However, what matters most for me is what a leader takes to bed with herself or himself, what they feel like on their deathbed, a moment each person faces alone, even when they are surrounded by loved ones. What I am talking about here are the values that should inform the decisions we take as leaders and how we deal with colleagues and other people.

It's those values that, in the words of movie actor and director Sidney Poitier, can send us to bed comfortably and make us courageous enough to face our end with character.

To make progress, societies need more leaders who go to bed comfortably and have the courage to face the end of their lives with character.

**NHLANHLA NENE**

Former Minister of Finance

*Photo: Courtesy of Thebe Investments Corporation*

# INTRODUCTION

'Once you make your first million dollars, the second million becomes inevitable,' Canadian-American motivational speaker Brian Tracy says. 'It is not becoming a millionaire that is important, it is the person you must become to become a millionaire. You have to become a completely different person beyond 99% of the people in the world. You have to develop honesty, discipline, quality relationships, ability to set priorities and so on. Once you develop these qualities as you earn your first million dollars, getting that second million becomes much easier.'

There are two reasons why I find this quote so apt and compelling. First, I have found it to be true even when it comes to writing books. Putting together my first book, *Masters of Money: Strategies for Success from the CFOs of South Africa's Biggest Companies*, was a difficult mission. Conceiving the idea, securing the publisher, reaching out for interviews, writing the content and sourcing imagery felt like trekking across a series of rocky trails through a rugged landscape. However, once I developed the qualities to surmount these obstacles, writing a second book became inevitable.

The second reason I love this quote is that it speaks to a key reason why you should read this book. It aims to divulge some of the main characteristics of South Africa's top business leaders. I seek to uncover the CEO X factor – those unique personality traits, values and business principles that have made them the dynamos they are.

The CEOs featured here have all developed the required character to become the dollar millionaires Brian Tracy has in mind. They are all accomplished individuals who are highly paid for the work they do. For example, publicly available annual financial statements show that despite pandemic-related financial dips, Momentum Metropolitan's Jeanette Marais, Nampak's Erik Smuts and Harmony's Peter Steenkamp all earned well over a million rand a month in the 2022 financial year. The three most jaw-dropping annual packages are from Vodacom's Shameel Joosub, Capitec's Gerrie Fourie and Motus's Osman Arbee, who received R54 million,[3] R33 million[4] and R48 million,[5] respectively.

In his book *Take Charge*, General Electric Southern Africa's CEO, Nyimpini Mabunda, writes that 'billionaires get the same 24 hours that the rest of us do, they are just much smarter at using their time than we are'.

They may be intelligent by nature but much of what they have achieved is thanks to first-hand experience, a level of emotional intelligence and a willingness to learn. Beyond wits, they have developed certain attributes that enable them to lead South Africa's most successful companies and on top of that earn so well. It is these attributes that I have sought to identify and document.

CEOs of major companies generally wield considerable power. Take for example the accounting scandal involving Steinhoff's former CEO Markus Jooste, which led to a 93% decline in the company share price and hundreds of job losses. As former chairman of the company, Christo Wiese reportedly lost R125 billion[6] as a result of the fraudulent activities that were exposed in late 2017. In an interview for the Showmax miniseries *Steinheist*, Christo repeatedly blames Markus for his misfortunes.

A less depressing example of the kind of influence wielded by CEOs is that of Chris van der Merwe, founding CEO of the Curro group of schools and Stadio tertiary institutions. The two companies have not only provided a platform for affordable, high-quality education but have also created many jobs. Curro is the leading for-profit independent schools provider in South Africa, with over 70 000 learners today[7] while Stadio provides higher education to close to 40 000 students.[8]

Then there is Edward Kieswetter, commissioner of the South African Revenue Services (SARS) and President of the Da Vinci Institute. Edward made a name for himself as the CEO who turned around Alexander Forbes when the company was found guilty of combining its cash assets with those of other funds to attract interest, a practice known as bulking. In my interview with him, he describes the leadership lessons he learnt at Alexander Forbes and what he has done to restore order and integrity at SARS after the institution fell victim to state capture.

Each leader in this book can write their own book; in fact, some have already done so. However, such books tend to offer only that individual's perspective from working in a handful of organisations and in a limited number of industries. *The CEO X factor* brings together the lessons, advice and thinking of the country's most successful business minds from a variety of companies and a wide range of industries, thereby providing a much broader perspective. My approach has been to ask the CEOs what they consider to be the secret to success and then seeking practical examples of how they have applied these principles in their organisations.

For example, Peermont's Nigel Atherton's secret is the ability to *re-invent* himself when the need arises, while Momentum Metropolitan's Jeanette Marais says you must ensure that the goals you focus on are of an *infinite* nature. Vukani Mngxati of Accenture shows how *inclusivity* is critical to business strategy and Motus's Osman Arbee shares a real-life success story of how allowing *flexibility* in the company's strategy ensured a comeback after the COVID-19 pandemic. Gerrie Fourie explains how Capitec has mastered the principle of *simplicity* to outperform more established banks.

Both Thomas Kgokolo, who headed South African Airways through its transition from business rescue, and the former CEO of Sanlam Emerging Markets, JJ Ngulube, explain why *courage* enabled them to succeed in their different missions. The former CEO of WDB Investments, Faith Khanyile, and the CEO of Discovery Health, Ryan Noach, agree that finding *balance* breeds success. Faith says CEOs must balance having bold strategies with having achievable goals, while Ryan asserts that a strategy should be complicated enough that others cannot copy it but simple enough that you and your team can implement it.

Some CEOs cannot pinpoint a single X factor but instead defer to a set of rules that they apply in their pursuit of commercial triumphs. Edward Kieswetter from SARS has crafted what he calls the *six I's*, while Harmony's Peter Steenkamp has his own fascinating set of *nine commandments*. Busi Mavuso, who leads Business Leadership South Africa, firmly believes in Colin Powell's *40–70 decision-making* rule and Sandra Crous of PaySpace explains why, for her, the secret to success lies in Malcolm Gladwell's *10 000 hours* rule.

For some CEOs it is all about the attitude you have while running point from the corner office. For Vodacom's Shameel Joosub you need a *battler mentality*, Leila Fourie of the Johannesburg Stock Exchange believes in a *climber's mindset* and IDF's Polo Leteka speaks to having a *teachable spirit*. Mteto Nyati encourages *vulnerability*, General Electric's Nyimpini Mabunda advocates for *taking ownership* and Chris van der Merwe from Curro has a detailed dossier on how *humility* has been key to his success.

Sandile Zungu and Isaac Shongwe are two African industrialists who have faced significant challenges as they define the face of black business in post-apartheid South Africa. Separately, they explain how forming the right *relationships* and viewing business as a *catalyst for social good* leads to both individual and communal success. In the professional services sector, EY's Ajen Sita demonstrates the importance of *company culture*, Webber Wentzel's Sally Hutton talks about the need for *multi-pronged solutions* and PwC Africa's Territory Senior Partner Dion Shango professes that authenticity and integrity combined, a concept called *authentegrity*, is the only way forward for the accounting profession.

When I met Nedbank's CEO, Mike Brown, I got the sense that he was not only a person who believes in finding one's *purpose*, but has also found his. Similarly, Tourvest's Sean Joubert has found his niche now that he is working in an industry that has *alignment* to what he is passionate about after a laborious stint at DiData. While technology didn't really make Sean's heart skip a beat, the recent CEO of Exxaro Mxolisi Mgojo believes it is a necessary tool for *innovation*, which is, in his view, the X factor organisations need to thrive in the modern era.

'You need to have a good *understanding* of the different personalities on your team and to know what motivates them, what influences them and also what is going on in their personal lives,' says Rui Morais of Dis-Chem. Erik Smuts, CEO of Nampak, reads from a similar script, explaining that understanding between staff members builds *trust*, which then becomes a multiplication factor because leaders let team members work without interruption and team members are comfortable with the direction their leaders are taking them in. At RMB, CEO Emrie Brown believes that success comes from having the *right team* 'on the bus', while Bidvest's Mpumi Madisa says the team must foster *cohesion* to excel.

The 31 CEOs in this book are stellar individuals who all have captivating stories about how they became captains of industry. They stem from a wide variety of backgrounds: impoverished overpopulated townships like Thembisa, Umlazi, Laudium and Soweto, bucolic surroundings like Seshego, Tabase, Kwa-Biyela and Rolle, and the leafy suburbs of Northcliff, Victory Park, Goodwood and Bloemfontein. While all but one of the CFOs in *Masters of Money* studied accounting, the CEOs in this book have a range of academic backgrounds including agriculture, social science, engineering, actuarial science, economics, medicine, mining and law.

In speaking to these money makers, I have also learnt a whole lot about business in South Africa and I hope that you will find it as insightful. Apart from describing some of the characteristics required to lead a successful company, *The CEO X factor* also offers interesting information on the motor industry three-year cycle, the making of a fully digital mine, the can-versus-glass war, hotel management contract complexities, busy but unprofitable airline routes, tech hackathons, the economic effect of contagion, and much more.

May this book leave you as inspired as I was. When you are done reading it, head over to www.kcrottok.com to receive your CEO X factor certificate.

## KC ROTTOK CHESAINA

MTN, ALTRON & BSG's **Mteto Nyati**
*(Photo: Courtesy of Altron)*

# MTETO NYATI

*Betting on Excellence*

If leaders do not talk about their own faults, they give the
impression that they're perfect, which makes people think that they
have all the answers – yet they don't.'[9]

I first met Mteto Nyati in August 2020 – at his home – when, as organiser
of the SA Professional Services Awards, I presented him with a Lifetime Achievement Award for excellence in management. We had just
emerged from the first hard COVID-19 lockdown and still had to wear
masks, which made our interaction somewhat awkward. Still, I could
gather even from our brief engagement the aura of a leader who consistently inspires his charges.

It was for that reason that he was at the top of the list of CEOs
I wanted to interview for this book. I eventually managed to pin him
down for a chat one evening in July 2022, shortly after his farewell
party at Altron, a company he had joined in April 2017. My first question was what he planned to do now that he was 'retired'.

He laughed and said he had invested in a few medium-size companies.

'Are they start-ups?' I wondered.

'Not at all,' he replied. 'I realised a long time ago that I'm not an
entrepreneur; I'm not the kind of person to conceptualise something.
Rather, I'm the type who gets into something that already exists and
makes it better. The companies I've invested in are in advertising and
data analytics. I will participate in their management, which means
I will have to limit my other board seats to only three other companies.'

Months after our interview, in November 2022, Business Systems

Group (BSG) announced that Mteto had acquired a 40% stake in the company. BSG is a 25-year-old business and technology consulting firm founded by Greg Reis. With his investment, Mteto replaced Reis as executive chairman.

Mteto has a long history in leadership positions. He served as the CEO of MTN South Africa from March 2014 to March 2017, following his position as chief enterprise officer of the group. This was after his time at two software giants – first as a director of global technology services for South and Central Africa at IBM, and then as managing director at Microsoft South Africa between 2008 and 2014.

After their retirement, many CEOs sit down to write their memoirs. Mteto ticked this off his list in 2019 already, when *Betting on a Darkie – Lifting the Corporate Game* was published. The book is a telltale account of his life, starting with his upbringing as the son of a shopkeeper in Tabase in the Eastern Cape.

As a child, Mteto was, to his own admission, naughty. Towards the end of his primary school years, his mother discovered that he and his friends got high on inhaling petrol they had stolen. His brother also told on him for smoking second-hand cigarette butts. These revelations got him a proper hiding and he was packed off to boarding school.

Even at university Mteto was a 'poster child for irresponsibility'. He ended up having a son with a medical student, and someone he knew from his high school days, and a daughter with a BCom student. 'My actions almost derailed the studies of two talented people,' he writes in his book. 'It pains me when I cast my mind back to this period of my life.'

I tell him I was surprised by how forthcoming he is about his own shortcomings. 'I'm an honest person and I felt it was important to include that information in my book to show people that there is nothing special about me,' he explains. 'People need to know that I did not grow up as a model citizen. I draw parallels to Barack Obama who, for example, was a chain smoker but ended up as arguably one of America's greatest presidents.

'If leaders do not talk about their own faults, they give the impression that they're perfect, which makes people think that they have all the answers – yet they don't. Creating an environment where you are honest about your imperfections shows that you are open to be persuaded by views that are different from your own.'

## Telling it like it is

Mteto is indeed fiercely honest in his book. For example, he is critical about how the IBM management tried to recruit him for the role of CEO behind the back of the incumbent. He also writes about how a director at Eskom, who he names in the book, attempted to solicit a bribe in the process of awarding a contract, and how MTN wanted to downplay the reasons for his departure when he left the mobile communication giant for Altron.

Mteto is frank: he decided early on that he was not going to ask anyone for their permission to write about them. He intended to be honest about events as he recalled them, he explains. 'If someone wanted to challenge me in court, then so be it. They could claim that I wrote something that didn't happen and call me a liar, but so far, nobody has made such claims. I suppose there are people who are uncomfortable about the things I wrote, but ultimately it's my story and my truth.'

The book contains several testimonials from people who've worked with Mteto over the course of his career. 'I wanted to include other people's views because I'm generally uncomfortable talking about myself; I prefer others to give me their perspective,' he says. 'So I asked a few people to write about me. All I gave them was the preferred length, nothing else. And I did not change what they submitted to me.'

Dingulwazi Makwelo, who worked in the IT support division at Altron, contributed to a chapter. His initial take on Mteto was of an astute businessman with little empathy for staff, someone who cares only about the bottom line. However, Mteto's emphasis on taking people's feelings into account to inform decisions convinced him otherwise. 'With his unique and modern approach, he makes you feel appreciated and valuable no matter what position or and status you hold,' Makwelo writes.

Each chapter in the book opens with an appropriate quote. If you follow Mteto on LinkedIn, you will notice that he frequently posts quotes aimed at not only encouraging people but also challenging them to excel. 'At almost every meeting I go to, there will be at least one person who tells me how they wake up to my quotes and what impact it has on their day. Although that wasn't my intention when I started sharing these quotes, it's become a way in which I can help shape people's lives.'

### Tempting parking spaces

My favourite quote in his book is one by Will Rogers, an American tongue-in-cheek social commentator. 'The road to success has many tempting parking places,' he says. I asked Mteto about the parking spots of his career.

'When I go back to the village [Tabase] and look for the people I grew up with, many of my peers are not doing well. In fact, carrying on with negative behaviour has cost several their life. That could have been a parking space I might never have gotten out of had my mother not pointed me in the right direction.'

Being at IBM South Africa for close to 12 years, Mteto didn't realise that he was parked in a comfortable spot. 'I should have realised earlier that the promises of my becoming CEO would not come through in good time. It's important not to let your loyalty stifle your growth. Leaving IBM accelerated my career growth, which made me realise I would have been much further had I left sooner.'

Although he was very successful during his time at Microsoft and leaving the company was difficult, he realised, though, that if he had stayed, he would have missed out on valuable lessons learnt at Altron. 'Altron is a listed company with high demands from investors. In contrast, the Microsoft business was well supported by funders in the US. If I'd stayed, I would never have developed the expertise to deal with the kind of liquidity problems I found at Altron.'

In all the positions Mteto has held, he's shown that a leader's primary responsibility is that of stewardship. It is about ensuring that management takes care of everything they're the custodians of, and when they hand it over one day, it has to be in a better shape than what they had found it in. This is one of the principles along which he shapes his career.

'I don't think I would have had the impact I had at MTN without the experiences at Microsoft and IBM. Each new assignment I've taken on has been progressively harder than the one before, but each prior role was necessary for me to be able to tackle the issues in a new position.

'For example, MTN was my first encounter with investors in a listed company, and I came to appreciate how important people are in the success of companies. It is critical to give them a voice to shape and execute strategies.'

Strategy, Mteto believes, should be based on practical insight gained from customers. For example, at Altron he realised that the buying behaviour of their customers was changing. They were cutting down on the number of suppliers they dealt with and buying more from the ones they retained. This meant that a client would develop a strategic relationship with a certain supplier, which they then would give lots of business to and consequently demand bigger discounts.

He was concerned that customers would shy away from the group, which was seen as a collection of different, largely independent companies. Altron therefore changed its strategy to consolidate its offerings under a single umbrella as part of a strategy Mteto called One Altron.

### The power of engineer CEOs
At MTN, Mteto also gained valuable insights from customers. When he first took over, the company was embroiled in a long-standing dispute with striking workers. The only cartoon in Mteto's memoir is a hilarious illustration by Jeremy Nell, showing an MTN executive pacing about in his office with his cell phone and saying, 'Sorry, I can't hear

you ... move around.' On the other end of the line is a workers' representative, also on his phone and standing among *toyi-toying* staffers, asking, 'Do you have a landline on which we can call you?'

'At MTN, my mission became personal,' Mteto says. 'When I took the job, my entire family had Vodacom lines and we all switched to MTN sim cards one weekend. It was like we disappeared off the face of the earth because we lost connectivity. My wife and daughter kept asking me what I got them into!

'I realised we needed to focus on customer experience, and today MTN has the best network coverage in the country. In many companies, you may have someone sitting behind a computer who wants to serve customers, but the systems are not helping them. Even simple things like your website need to be enhanced to improve your customers' experience if you hope to be successful.'

Mteto is trained as an engineer and he believes many engineers would make good CEOs if they stepped out of their comfort zone and considered transitioning to leadership roles. Engineers are problem solvers, he says, and the kind of problems they generally have to handle require a dynamic approach. For example, an engineer can design a bridge in one place, but if he wanted to design a similar bridge in a different place with different wind patterns, he would have to adapt his design accordingly.

Many engineers are also introverts, and although it's often assumed that extroverts make good CEOs, Mteto believes the opposite is true. He says introverts generally do not want to draw attention to themselves and so tend to give credit to others – which is what most teams need. They also often thrive on validation, which could have a positive impact on their performance.

Lastly, he says engineers have the ability to connect the dots; they can read a situation from looking at only a few data points, whereas someone from a different profession may need much more information to come to the same conclusion.

## *Challenging perceptions*

'Betting on a darkie' was a provocative title for his book. And it was intentional – Mteto has been an advocate of highlighting black excellence throughout his career. The term – generally considered derogatory – made people sit up. Mteto takes issue with the perception among some that black corporate professionals are lazy or not as clever as their white counterparts. The book's title is a challenge to its readers to recognise that no one group can monopolise excellence.

'Many people from other races think their success should be attributed solely to their own efforts and fail to recognise that they're a product of opportunities that their would-be competitors from other races did not have. I think my story is an example of what a person of colour can do if given the chance, and that their excellence will shine through.'

I asked him about his take on whether leadership is a matter of 'nature' or 'nurture'. He doesn't believe it's one or the other, he muses. 'Some people are natural leaders, but most are made into leaders. You could be born a leader, but because your circumstances have prevented you from developing certain competencies you might fail to become the great leader you were born to be.'

Whether a born or a made leader, the ability to make decisions is key when you're at the helm of a company. In making decisions, Mteto prioritises fairness and consistency. He also aligns all decisions to his personal values and those of the organisation. Many decisions have not been easy. At Microsoft, for example, he encouraged all managers to hire people who were different from them – race, gender or age – to achieve greater diversity. So, if a manager was a white, male Baby Boomer he was expected to hire blacks, millennials or white women.

In repositioning MTN, he divided the leadership team into three 'thought buckets'. One bucket was for positions that had to be cut to make the structure more streamlined. Another was for positions whose value had to reconsidered after 12 months. The third group he believed had the necessary abilities to execute the new strategy.

Creating One Altron was also a difficult call, as bringing together the different companies that made up the group meant that many executive positions would become redundant. But a drastic step like this was necessary to save the company since it was making heavy losses. As a result of this restructuring, Altron managed to grow and ended up employing more people than they had at the start.

'A leader should not be afraid to make tough decisions for the benefit of the company. I did not make decisions based on what is best for myself, but rather on what is best for the company. The attitude exuded by the leadership team is important. During COVID-19 we cut executive bonuses and shareholder dividends before even thinking of asking our employees to forego salary increases. We focused on being equitable rather than being equal, because the lower-level employees are the most vulnerable. They require greater financial protection than senior management.'

After less than two years leading Altron, the company was one of the top three on the Johannesburg Stock Exchange, with its shares having gained the most in an otherwise tough year. The group had been restored to profitability and was paying dividends for the first time in many years.

Mteto's long and illustrious career is ample proof that you can indeed 'bet on a darkie'.

# RYAN NOACH

*The doctor turned corporate leader*

'A strategy must be complicated enough that others can't copy it,
but simple enough that you can deliver. This balance between
simplicity and complexity is critical.'

'Is Rottok an Indian name?'

As soon as we're connected on our virtual call, Ryan Noach takes control. Built like a boxer – not quite what you'd expect a corporate executive to look like – he is ruggedly handsome, with a chiselled chin covered in a greying stubble.

'No,' I say, 'I'm from the Kalenjin tribe in Kenya.'

'I looked into your background earlier,' he responds. 'I thought you might be descended from the Indian traders who once lived in Kenya.'

'Have you been to the country?'

'Yes, many times,' he says. 'One of my closest friends is actually from there.'

Our comfortable back-and-forth is classic Ryan. He never goes into something unprepared, I find out as we talk, yet always makes it easy for people to be around him. 'I even took the time to check whether you're a Discovery customer. We wouldn't be having this conversation if you weren't … '

I laugh nervously, unsure whether he's joking or not.

'I appreciate your time,' I say, 'even if we only have an hour.'

'What do you mean by "only"?' he exclaims. 'Do you know how much you can accomplish in an hour? You can change the world in one hour.'

DISCOVERY HEALTH's **Ryan Noach**

*(Photo: Courtesy of Discovery)*

So I dive right in to make the most of our time. I enquire about the most memorable hours in his life. 'The most important one was my second wedding, because it created a life partnership with my wife, who is my greatest support and an emotional pillar of strength. The births of my children were obviously other memorable moments.'

On a professional level, graduating as a doctor was the realisation of Ryan's childhood ambition to become a physician. It was the culmination of many years' training and started his career in healthcare.

'For as long as I can remember I wanted to become a doctor. As a kid, I used to play with a doctor's toy set that included a stethoscope and a toy ambulance. Later I volunteered as a first aider and for various roles in emergency services. At high school, I sustained a bad rugby injury and the best way to stay with the team was to be a medic.'

Ryan became a doctor because he wanted to make a difference in people's lives – that has always defined his personal sense of value and impact. And in his role today, his impact reaches millions of people. Although he still misses medicine and the personal interaction with patients, he has an amplified ability to achieve his childhood dream of truly making a difference at the widest possible level.

### *Realising a dream*

Ryan was born in 1974 and attended King David Victory Park in Johannesburg, a Jewish school. He recognises that he grew up with an unfair advantage that gave him a much better chance at life than most people in South Africa, due to the apartheid system. After matriculating in 1991, he was accepted at the University of the Witwatersrand's medical school, from where he graduated in 1997.

Ryan also earned a specialist postgraduate diploma in primary emergency care, at the time the highest qualification available in emergency medicine, which qualified him to be an emergency room (ER) physician. When the government withdrew its subsidy for helicopter-based emergency services just more than 20 years ago, Ryan saw an opportunity for his first entrepreneurial venture. Together with some colleagues, they decided to privatise the service.

'I did many entrepreneurial things when I was at school and at university, but they were mostly for social good rather than for commercial gain,' Ryan explains. 'I took my cue from my dad, who was a dentist and volunteered alongside a team of paramedics to support emergency services. In 2001, a massive earthquake struck in India and more than 20 000 people died. There was a global call for assistance and together with a group of firefighters and rescue personnel from South Africa, we volunteered to help. There were about 60 of us and I led the medical component of the team.'

On their return, and given their success, they recognised there was an opportunity to formalise their effort for future – more organised – responses. And so they created Rescue South Africa, a not-for-profit organisation that still exists today and of which Ryan was the chairperson for some years.

In 2005, Ryan completed the Executive Development Programme at the Gordon Institute of Business Science because he wanted to understand basic finance and key business principles.

In their helicopter service business, Ryan and his colleagues worked closely with Netcare 911 and based on these interactions, he was appointed CEO of Netcare 911 in March 2003. Just two years later, Ryan rose to become the chief operating officer (COO) of the group. Netcare offered a fantastic learning experience; forming the foundation of his business understanding.

'I worked for an inspirational guy – the CEO and founder of Netcare, Jackie Shevel. His departure coincided with my promotion to the position of COO, but the new CEO was more institutionally orientated than entrepreneurial. For the first 18 months of his tenure, he also operated from the United Kingdom, so I didn't have the same direct contact that I enjoyed with Jackie. The combination of a poor working relationship and troubles in my first marriage culminated in my leaving the company in December 2006.'

At the time, Ryan vowed never to work for another corporate entity again. 'I went out on my own doing consulting work and various bits and pieces, some of which I still do today, such as Shesha Tuks, the first company in South Africa to offer licensed passenger transport via tuk tuks [three-wheel motorised rickshaws]. A friend and I founded the business as a social capital venture, and we now have a young entrepreneur running it. We are on the verge of selling our stake to an investment fund.'

During his time at Netcare, one of Ryan's most difficult jobs was negotiating tariffs with medical schemes. Negotiations with Discovery were by far the most difficult and sophisticated. His talks with them were so intense that the two parties had to meet on neutral territory, a hotel somewhere halfway between their two offices.

Through those discussions, he gained great respect for, and later became friends with, the then CEO of Discovery Health, Neville Koopowitz, who is today the CEO of Discovery's UK business. Koopowitz and his right-hand man, Dr Jonathan Broomberg, tried to recruit Ryan, but he was adamant that he wanted to stay out of the corporate world. However, eventually they convinced him to join the company as a consultant, which he did in mid-2008 and a year later, he accepted the COO role at Discovery Health.

Over the years Ryan has found that leadership is a series of learned behaviours, instincts and aptitudes – which he's crafted into his own leadership style. He points out that doctors have to act as leaders in their daily work. For example, when he worked as a trauma specialist, he would coordinate a team of medical staff when they had to resuscitate a patient.

What lacks in that environment is commercial leadership and business skills. Through executive coaching, various mentorships and many leadership books, Ryan has managed to bridge that gap.

'Relationships are important,' he observes. 'You have to inspire and motivate people to transform their thinking and their performance. My boss [Discovery founder] Adrian Gore is a visionary who has changed the medical schemes industry in South Africa and the approach to wellness around the world. He created a concept of shared value that

[American academic] Michael Porter teaches at the Harvard Business School. The way that Adrian does it is by giving people a purpose and inspiring and motivating them. It's astoundingly amazing, and I find it a privilege to be a part of it.'

### Change leadership

In January 2020, mere weeks before the COVID-19 pandemic would send the world into lockdown, Ryan took over as CEO of Discovery Health. So far, his tenure has been nothing like he'd expected, and it has been defined by how Discovery, as one of the leading healthcare organisations in South Africa, has had to respond to the pandemic. It was a tragic time; they lost 17 000 customers and 24 staff members.

If there was a silver lining during this time, it was that it gave the healthcare system an opportunity to reinvent itself in some ways and offered Ryan a chance to define his leadership style.

According to Ryan, a change in how people use healthcare counts among the many things that have changed dramatically. For example, a lot of care that was handled in hospital before now happens outside. Furthermore, wasteful expenditure in the healthcare system has dropped substantially, because people refrain from going to hospital for every small ache and pain. These days they rather treat themselves or consult their general practitioner.

There has also been an uptake in digitisation, with greater engagement with digital tools, telemedicine, remote care, remote monitoring and digital therapeutics – things the global industry struggled to get people in healthcare settings to engage with before the pandemic.

COVID-19 also highlighted the need to focus on mental healthcare, which Ryan described in an op-ed in *Business Day* 'as the sting in the tail of the pandemic', having left us with anxiety and a sense of isolation and loneliness. The change in the way we work, the lack of social connectedness and particularly children being kept out of school have had a massive impact on mental well-being, reflected in Discovery's data showing a surge in cases of depression and anxiety.

The global health crisis changed everything, and Discovery innovated to help protect the lives of their clients. For example, they made arrangements with hotels where clients could go to isolate. They also sent them equipment to treat themselves at home and to help monitor for early signs of deterioration when hospital beds were full.

In addition, Discovery changed the benefits of the scheme's plans to cater for the funding they needed and built an information hub that became a go-to source of reliable information about COVID-19 in the country. 'We created information sharing structures, webinars and other things where doctors could learn new stuff about COVID and talk to colleagues. Our psychosocial support groups allowed medical staff to deal with burnout to difficult working conditions,' he says.

Discovery also worked with the government and others in the business community to roll out vaccinations nationally. They strategised with the health department on how to procure and distribute vaccines and got involved in educational campaigns. Anybody living in South Africa, whether a national citizen or not, could get vaccinated at a Discovery site. The company also implemented a mandatory vaccination policy for employees and, where required, provided financial support to them.

The pandemic redefined how Discovery interacts with doctors. Instead of fee-for-service payments it now works on a value-based payment model.

I ask Ryan to explain the difference.

'Say you go to hospital to have your appendix removed. In a fee-for-service world, you pay for the time spent in the theatre. We pay for the anaesthetics, the medicine you get, and the time in the ward. If you get a wound infection from the operation, we end up paying the healthcare providers more.

'However, in a value-based world, we pay the doctors and the hospitals to complete a successful appendicectomy with the best outcomes. If there are complications, it is at their risk. We are therefore aligning incentives around better outcomes. It's a reimbursement approach that shares risk and rewards better outcomes.'

Ryan believes companies that had a higher purpose did better during the pandemic than those that did not. Discovery's purpose is enhancing and protecting the lives of their clients and they tested every decision against that. 'It's not just about the words on the wall; it actually defines our culture and I think it's carried us through. We didn't focus only on the products; our purpose led us to do things a health insurer would typically never do, such as booking clients into hotels.'

'Hotels aren't cheap,' I remark. 'I can imagine that decision was not unanimously accepted when it was first suggested?'

'We have an interesting innovation principle at Discovery, which says we don't raise problems before we look at the opportunity. I'm the one who suggested using hotels to our team. They all thought I was crazy, but we explored it and did a deal with two hotel groups. The idea was that if somebody in your house was diagnosed with COVID-19, we would give you the opportunity to send either the patient to the hotel or the rest of the family to protect them. This is the embodiment of shared value. As an insurer, we didn't want the people around those who were infected to get sick, too, as that would only mean more sick people and even higher costs than the hotel bill.'

### Looking back to move forward

Discovery's analysis shows that the initial hard lockdown helped the country because it delayed severe illness in South Africa and allowed us to benefit from lessons learnt in Europe and America. As a consequence, we were able to treat patients better, with data showing we had much better survival rates during that phase of the pandemic than a city like New York and or a country like Italy. It's less clear how effective subsequent lockdowns were, the data shows.

'Are we done with COVID?' I ask.

'Definitely not,' Ryan says emphatically. 'Firstly, we still see COVID-19 cases every day. Today alone we have eight clients in ICU on mechanical ventilation because of COVID, so people are still getting sick.

'Over the course of the pandemic, the trajectory of complications and death has been downwards, and my hope is that it will continue that way. But as the virologists point out, we still face the risk of a new variant that could drive another severe outbreak or wave. In Singapore and in parts of America, they are currently dealing with new variants that can become virulent and will almost certainly reach us, too.'

Another concern is the number of people suffering from so-called Long COVID. 'We have seen a large proportion of people reporting signs and symptoms of enduring disease many months after infection. And then there are the mental health problems arising from the lockdowns, the anxiety, mask wearing and isolation.'

The pandemic seems not to have hit Africa as hard as other parts of the world, which some commentators attribute to the continent's large young population (even though this is a result of life expectancy on the continent being fairly short). That said, Ryan thinks there is gross underreporting of cases and severe illness across Africa.

In 2022, Discovery launched a health insurance product in five African markets – Kenya, Nigeria, Zambia, Mozambique and the Democratic Republic of Congo – and will be expanding to more markets in coming years.

'We need a well-developed supply side [hospitals and doctors] for our insurance products to thrive,' Ryan explains. 'In Africa, we adopted a watch-and-wait approach until we deemed the timing right for private health insurance to grow. We've seen many of our competitors get rather badly hurt financially on their African health insurance ventures and so we've been very strategic about our timing.'

### The secret to a winning strategy

When I ask Ryan what the elements of a good strategy are, he says he won't give me 'the business school answer' but rather something that is based on lived experience.

'I think the first part of a good strategy is one that is built by the people and supported by the team. As the CEO, it's easy to simply propose your own version of the strategy and tell everybody, "Here it is, go run with it." But that doesn't work. You need a strategy that the team has created, believes in and works together at to achieve.

'Secondly, you need some disruptive elements in a strategy. At Discovery we seek disruption in a considered and risk-mitigated way.

Thirdly, a strategy must be complicated enough that others can't copy it, but simple enough that you can deliver. This balance between simplicity and complexity is critical. And lastly, we are a purpose-driven organisation. Everything we do must be true to our purpose.'

'How would your colleagues describe you?' I ask.

'They'd probably say I am very tough, perhaps even difficult to work with. Yes, I have high expectations, but I'm also fair, and I'm willing to change my mind about stuff when presented with rational arguments. I'm easy to read, though – I wear my heart on my sleeve; I'm truly an emotionally charged person.'

'So, you can't play poker?'

'No, no, I'm a terrible poker player!' Ryan laughs.

'I think my colleagues would also say I'm an energetic and committed worker who can be unrealistic sometimes. I often push people to the point where they feel overstretched. A visionary leader must set unrealistic goals at times and then allow the system and the people to calibrate.

'Just look at my boss Adrian. At the age of 59 he has set a target of running a mile [1.6 km] in five minutes. It's an astounding challenge, because it's trying to achieve something close to the world record for a 60-year-old. The lesson is that no matter how tough and how unrealistic it might be, set the bar high and you could achieve what you previously thought was impossible.'

Ryan and his wife have a two-year-old baby who he longs to spend meaningful time with. He also aspires to build a strong relationship with his children from his previous marriage; an 18-year-old daughter studying actuarial science and 16-year-old twins who were in matric in 2022.

He loved being in the sky when he was involved with the helicopter emergency service. It took him a long time to find the financial means and time in his career to get his pilot licence, but for the past five years he has been in the cockpit himself.

As the precious hour of Ryan's time comes to a close, I work up the courage to ask him whether his muscular build has ever come in handy.

'Oh yes,' he says with a reminiscent smile. 'I earned some pocket money as a medical student working as a firefighter and nightclub bouncer.'

VODACOM & VODAFONE's **Shameel Joosub**
*(Photo: Courtesy of Vodacom)*

# SHAMEEL JOOSUB

*The telecom giant with a battler mentality*

'I have a battler mentality. Failure is not an option, but I will also not wallow
in my own success. Yesterday's results were yesterday's results, you have to look at
where tomorrow's results are going to come from.'

After completing his articles in 1994, a young and ambitious chartered accountant, Shameel Joosub, joined Vodacom in the General
Ledger and Budget Control division. So started a journey that would
eventually take him to the company's top spot. 'I've been here for 28
years. In accounting terms, you can call me a fully depreciated asset!'

Of course he is anything but that.

Shameel, who was born in Laudium, Pretoria in 1971, displayed business talent from an early age despite a tough childhood. His parents
had divorced by the time he learnt to walk, and life wasn't easy for him
and his siblings. By the age of five, he was trading with his brothers,
selling kites, marbles, samosas and toys in the neighbourhood.

At age seven, he would trek to Marabastad, the non-white market in
Pretoria, to buy sweets for ten cents, then head to the city centre where
he would shout 'Two bob! Two bob!' to passersby in pursuit of a hawk-
er's wage. In school he had a fully fledged business selling sweets and
even had other kids working for him; he had divided the playground into
zones that they would foray into during break time for a commission.

Despite him doing well in high school, Shameel's family could not
afford to send him to university. In 1989, he enrolled at the University
of South Africa to study accounting part time and signed a training contract with a medium-size audit firm. He continued his entrepreneurial

exploits by selling perfumes that his exiled uncle in London would send to him. A real paper chaser, he would also do book-keeping on weekends for small businesses.

Then, in 1994, Shameel started his professional career at Vodacom. Within a few years, he had moved into the financial management division and later to procurement. One day the then CEO of Vodacom walked into his office and asked him to look at an offer they had received to buy a large number of phones at a 30% discount. At the time, Vodacom didn't purchase and sell phones, but with Shameel's trading experience, he believed they could make a success of it. He sold off the phones within a day and, using his import experience from the perfume business, started bringing phones into the country. Vodacom Equipment was born and Shameel was appointed as managing director at the age of 26. The equipment model was so successful that Vodacom replicated it in other markets outside South Africa.

This got Shameel noticed. Vodacom South Africa's customer division, which was a separate unit from the network business, was running at a loss and when the managing director was relieved of his duties, Shameel was enlisted to turn it around. At age 29, he was allowed to do things his own way, which included restructuring the company to set it on the right trajectory. He revamped the distribution model and brought in the people with the right competencies, and within six months the division was profitable.

Within five years, the base of subscribers had grown from 2 million to 12.5 million. The network and consumer companies were merged, and Shameel was appointed CEO of the combined entity. This allowed him the freedom to make the changes he wanted, which were centred on investing in technology and distribution. Under his leadership Vodacom South Africa grew substantially between 2004 and 2010.

'In January 2011, I was due to take on the CEO role of Vodafone in Spain,' Shameel says. 'I was meant to be there for a three-year period to turn around the business, but then the position of Group CEO at Vodacom became vacant. A year after I had left for Madrid, I was asked to take over here and I've held this position until now.'

During the past decade Vodacom has grown substantially on all metrics, including revenue and net profit. Today the Vodacom Group has a subscriber base of 175 million, including Vodafone Egypt, which the company recently acquired.

Shameel ascribes much of his success to what he learnt from his mother, his role model. 'Nobody has ever died from hard work,' he recalls her saying. And ever since he was a young boy in Laudium, he has tackled everything he does with effort and passion. 'In my own head, I'm still a battler, so every day is a new fight.

'I am not one to bask in glory and I don't expect my team to bask in glory either. When we achieve something, we say, "Okay guys, well done" and look for the next achievement. If you create that energy and nurture it, it ensures continued success.'

### A culture of innovation

Our interview takes place in Shameel's corner office on the top floor of Vodacom Corporate Park in Midrand. We sit at an eight-seater board-room table, where he sits at the head and the group's head of media relations to his left. The walls are covered with framed certificates, family portraits and various magazine covers bearing Shameel's commanding likeness.

'We're creating an ambidextrous organisation, one that will focus on maximising the current opportunities on the one hand while finding new ones on the other,' he says. 'I believe leadership starts with surrounding yourself with like-minded people who can help you achieve your goals. Their thinking must be aligned to the purpose of the company, which for us is to connect for a better future. The problem I've seen in the corporate environment is that people are saying the right things but then do the opposite. This leads to failed leadership, because your team will sense that you're not living out the purpose.'

A CEO should also not be afraid to stick his neck out and drive changes or innovation. 'There will be many naysayers who will question you. For instance, investors will ask why you're experimenting with various things instead of focusing on maximising your current products. But these same investors will sell their shares if your profits are not growing in a couple of years. So you have to be visionary and anticipate what the next big thing is going to be.'

But to be successful, a company must have compelling products and services. 'You need to keep the fire going by seeking out new revenue opportunities,' he advises. 'This is what we're doing with financial services on the continent – building a platform that will cater for everything from transfers to lending. We're taking decisions today that will properly set us up for the future.'

It's this culture of innovation that has led to Vodacom's annual hackathon, during which, for two days, separate teams each work on a new idea or concept they had thought up and then present it as a working prototype. The teams are from different countries and are made up of employees from different divisions, including operations, marketing, technology and finance. The winning prototype is then scaled to work in that specific organisation.

In 2022, 80 teams participated in the hackathon. What would typically take months in a normal corporate setup is compressed into 48 hours during this event. Great ideas are born and it creates camaraderie among the employees.

Leaders should always strive to develop people, Shameel observes. As the organisation grows, they must encourage employees to grow and progress along their career path by obtaining further qualifications, to make the best of internal opportunities, and to have appropriate promotion prospects and the like. The bar should constantly be raised to reach the next level at both an organisational and personal level. This involves encouraging employees to pursue learning opportunities and investing time to close skill gaps.

Shameel also believes in creating social contracts with governments and to avoid working at cross-purposes with the national leadership. This means making the right calls, even if it means sacrificing short-term revenue. He cites an example of the company dropping charges for mobile money transactions in Kenya during the COVID-19 pandemic after talks with the Central Bank of Kenya. It cost the group over a billion rand in lost revenue but helped to ease the financial pressure on businesses during lockdowns – and upheld their reputation for supporting their customers to create a better future.

## *Learning from experience*

Among the highlights of Shameel's career are the positions he held at a young age. The first CEO he worked for was not even aware that he was only 26 when he was made managing director. 'He latched onto it, though, and told everyone, "You see how we promote youth in this company!"' Shameel laughs.

'My advice to young professionals is this: when you start a job and they ask you to do X, don't only do X; do X, Y and Z. You should also think outside the box, challenge the status quo and ask questions. Aim to do more than just what your job specs ask; try to figure out how different pieces can fit together. This is how I progressed from MD of Vodacom Equipment to CEO of Vodacom South Africa and on to CEO of Vodafone Spain and finally my current position of Group CEO.'

Shameel also celebrates what Vodacom has achieved as a company with regard to the growth in their subscriber base, as well as the launches of 3G, 4G and 5G networks. He is proud of the social path the group has taken and says it touches his heart to play a role in digital inclusion, rolling out mobile money in Africa and programmes to support charity. In every country where Vodacom has a presence, there is much to celebrate. In South Africa, for example, the company took responsibility for the end-to-end management of the vaccine roll-out, meaning that their platform supported everything from vaccine registrations to setting appointments and sending out confirmation messages.

'I'm also extremely proud of the number of people we have managed to grow and who have become formidable leaders in their own right, and the transformation I've seen in Vodacom. When I joined, the company was 95% white; today 76% of our employees are black because of investing in skills development. The executive committees comprise more than 50% black staff. We still have work to do on the gender side to increase our female component from 36% to 50%, but we are making progress on that front.'

Shameel has to think a while when I ask him about lows in his career. After a few moments, he mentions that Vodafone India offered him their CEO position in 2007, but that he had turned it down. He often wonders if it was the right decision because it could have accelerated his career progression. 'I ended up as CEO of the Vodacom Group, so I landed in the right place in the end, but maybe I took the long way around in getting here? There are always things that you could have done quicker and there are always lessons to be learnt. One thing I know now is that if something is not working, you need to pivot quickly and focus on something else.'

From a company perspective, he says there are also things that they could have done sooner, such as focusing on financial services in South Africa. 'We should have changed some things, like getting the right people in key positions, making structural adjustments and doing acquisitions. We have learnt to cut our losses early, for example making the call to switch off the MPESA mobile money service in South Africa, which was built on the wrong platform. The reason for its success in Kenya is that it's a largely non-banked environment, but expecting it to work in a banked society like South Africa was ambitious.'

In South Africa, the launch of the VodaPay super app in October 2021 exceeded expectations when it attracted 1.4 million downloads and 1 million registered users in its first three months. Shameel sees VodaPay as a precursor to MPESA's evolution and further strengthening Vodacom's fintech position across the group's footprint.

'The learning from the MPESA experience is this: bring in the right skills when you are launching something new, rather than simply deploying someone from your existing workforce to manage that product. We recently set up a company to manage our towers and the temptation was to use a good person from our team to run it. However, we decided we needed to employ someone who understood tower companies, who can then train up our own staff and manage the teams in future.'

Shameel says that when you take up opportunities 'you have to pay the school fees', but that you should leverage that experience and build your team around it. 'Our style is that if we see something that is great, we create dedicated focus to embark on it.

'For example, with big data, we saw the trend and so we went out and sourced the people who understood it and let them build the team. Three years later, the stuff that's coming out of that initiative is amazing simply because we ring-fenced that investment and gave it the space and budget needed to yield results.'

### Shameel, the strategist

Shameel lives by the saying 'but for the grace of God, they go higher'. This kind of thinking keeps him anchored, he says. 'I try for things never get to my head and show respect to everyone, from the person making tea to the different CEOs we have in the group. I believe in being passionate in both what you do and how you do it, galvanising teams and having a focus to achieve your goal.'

Still, making painful decisions is an undeniable part of his job. For example, when a new product is created something else must often be sacrificed. 'There will always be people asking why we're channelling money away from, say, building additional base stations to support a new venture,' he explains. 'The existing business will always have demands, so you need to be deliberate in innovation and think ahead.'

Many of his team members are surprised by how pedantic he can be when it comes to looking at the detail. He knows when to go deep and when to step back and guide. He's also not unwilling to accept unimpressive results when short-term pain will lead to long-term gain. Making that distinction arises from his ability to strike a balance. His early career as an entrepreneur has taught him about taking risks, while his training as an accountant gives him an understanding of the numbers.

'I have a battler mentality. Failure is not an option, but I will also not wallow in my own success. Yesterday's results were yesterday's results; you have to look at where tomorrow's results are going to come from. My immediate focus is the integration of our Egyptian acquisition and making sure that our foray into Ethiopia is a success. We are also building up our fibre capabilities and ensuring we have rural coverage.'

One of the things Shameel has spearheaded in Vodacom is the concept of reimagining problems. For example, when the company doesn't have enough capital to do something, they can either accept it as a limitation and watch someone else take up the opportunity or try to find a way to have a slice of the pie.

This situation is evident when it comes to rural coverage, which is a problem for telecommunication companies around the world. Shameel points out that Vodacom cannot live out its purpose of connecting for a better future if people in the most remote parts of society remain without network coverage. The company has therefore sourced development funding with the promise to pay the partners out of a shared-revenue model.

'Another example is fibre to homes and businesses,' he continues. 'We exist to connect people and we have to do that whether it is above the ground, under the ground or from outer space. In this regard, we've gone into joint ventures with external partners who will be off the balance sheet, because we'd rather own 50% of something than 100% of nothing.'

'We keep asking ourselves how we can scale our platforms to do good, including our mezzanine and financial services platforms. An example is to foster an investment culture by encouraging people to save more. MPESA Africa illustrates this impact, as we're using the lessons and successes from Kenya to roll out suitable platforms in other countries. The Kenyan government has launched a Hustler Fund to give small loans to businesses, which are paid out through MPESA. Furthermore, we have launched MPESA GO, a financial product for the youth [people between 10 and 17 years old] that will improve their digital money management and increase financial literacy.'

Shameel believes that strategy needs to come from the bottom up, with conversations starting at team level. These conversations should contribute to the operational strategy and inform how things should be done.

As a company that operates in multiple markets, Vodacom prefers to experiment with something in one market, make a success of it and then replicate it elsewhere. In 2020, for example, Vodacom partnered with Alipay, the digital payment provider of China's Alibaba Group, to launch the VodaPay super app, which allows South Africans to shop online, pay bills and send mobile money. In line with their preferred strategy, the group will first try to make a success of it in one market before rolling it out to the rest of the continent.

## Away from the office

Shameel is inspired by the life and work of the late former president Nelson Mandela. Prophet Muhammad is a religious icon for him, and he admires how the prophet lived his life with honesty and humility. As a father of three, and who recently became a grandfather, Shameel founded an orphanage that already made a difference to the lives of over 1 000 children.

Despite his very busy schedule, he reads extensively and has completed both an MBA through the University of Southern Queensland in Australia and the Advanced Management Programme at Harvard University. He loves to keep fit and when he gets bored of the treadmill, he competes with his friends in the pool or gets stuck into dance-based exercise. He once surprised the audience during the Vodacom CEO Awards when he starred in a remake of the Michael Jackson silhouette moonwalking across the stage.

That's Shameel Joosub, a man with a deft touch, from the boardroom to the ballroom.

# MPUMI MADISA

*A problem solver who makes things add up*

'Business is a lot like maths, which was my undergraduate degree.
To make a sale, you have to figure out what the customer value proposition is
and then work back to solve for it.'

When the news of Mpumi Madisa's appointment as the CEO of Bidvest broke in March 2019, there were plenty of naysayers. She was set to become the first female CEO of a company listed in the coveted Top 40 of the Johannesburg Stock Exchange. Some said it must be because there was something very wrong at Bidvest and that they had found a suitable scapegoat to pin it on when the corporate colossus came tumbling down. Others questioned the wisdom of Bidvest founder Brian Joffe in handing over the reins to a woman who's almost the same age as his 38-year-old company, and who didn't fit the profile of the usual big-company CEO.

Although Mpumi knew that she was being groomed to take over, the extent to which her appointment dominated business news still surprises her. It put her under immense pressure to perform and silence the critics, a challenge that was compounded by the advent of the COVID-19 pandemic. She has beaten the odds: under her leadership, the diversified industrial group has seen profits soar and managed to pay the biggest dividend to its shareholders in seven years in 2022.

'I was prepared to lead this organisation because I had been here for over a decade when my appointment was announced,' Mpumi says. 'I'd been on the board of directors for many years and knew the

BIDVEST's **Mpumi Madisa**
*(Photo: Courtesy of Bidvest)*

different teams quite well. Had I come in from a different organisation, without understanding the nuances of this business, I would perhaps have struggled to build credibility. Instead, I was ready to hit the ground running.

'I think the period between the announcement and my officially taking over in October 2020 was too long. That said, in those 18 months I had the opportunity to talk to the different divisions and get their views on what future they anticipated and how I could support them to reach their goals. It's worked out well, and I think my appointment has changed the minds of many boards out there who were hesitant to appoint a black woman to an executive role like this.'

Mpumi is right. In October 2021, her namesake Mpumi Zikalala was appointed to take over the CEO role at Kumba Iron Ore from January 2022. A month earlier, Clicks had announced that Bertina Engelbrecht will take over as CEO from Vikesh Ramsunder. In the same year, Nombasa Tsengwa was named to take over the top spot at Exxaro Resources a few months later.

### Carving a career path

Born in 1979 in Randfontein, Johannesburg, Mpumi was the only girl in a family of three children. She became the 'big sister' when her older brother passed away when they were still toddlers. Her school years were spent at Sancta Maria Junior School in Vanderbijlpark and Mondeor High School, from where she matriculated in 1997. Missing the submission deadline to apply for medical studies at the University of the Witwatersrand (Wits) derailed her hope to become a doctor somewhat, but she enrolled for a Bachelor of Science instead, with a plan to channel back to Medicine after a year.

Her first year at university was an eye-opener. Having to dissect rats during Biology practicals, she realised she couldn't handle the sight of blood. She accepted that while she wanted to become a doctor, she did not have the practical fortitude for it, and instead focused on the economics and mathematics courses that were part of her degree. She graduated in 2001 and joined Hollard Insurance a year later as a trainee marketing assistant. While at Hollard, she completed her honours degree in economics at Wits part time and joined Prestige Cleaning Services, a subsidiary of Bidvest, in 2003.

At Prestige, Mpumi moved up the corporate ladder quickly. Within months she was appointed general manager of client relations, a position that formed part of the executive committee (Exco), just one level below the board of directors.

'My personal anthem at the time was 'Beat It' by Michael Jackson,' Mpumi chuckles. 'I could not be defeated on any technical aspects of my role. It helped me rise through the ranks, but I didn't know enough about business to understand the other roles in the Exco. So I couldn't ask the operations director or CFO or human resources manager questions or make suggestions; I simply did not have the skill, depth or experience to contribute meaningfully to matters outside of my responsibilities.'

Mpumi discussed this discomfort with a friend, who suggested that she finds a job in government because joining another private entity would simply 'be doing the same thing, but expecting different results'. So she took up the role of Chief Director of Transformation at the Gauteng Department of Agriculture and Rural Development. As this was a new position, she had the freedom to draft her own policy, recruit her own team and execute her own strategy, which gave her end-to-end experience of a functioning unit.

In the run-up to the national elections in 2009, service delivery slowed as the leadership at most government levels focused on securing a renewed mandate. This really frustrated Mpumi and she was starting to consider opportunities outside the public sector. When she ran into the then CEO of Prestige Cleaning, Danie Otto, one day and he asked if she'd consider coming back, she did not hesitate. But, she said, on two conditions: she would not take up her previous role and she would be responsible for her own portfolio. Danie accepted both conditions and Mpumi rejoined the company as corporate affairs director, responsible for transformation, sustainability, marketing and client relations.

After 18 months, Mpumi was appointed head of group sales and marketing to help stem the continued decline in revenues at Prestige. She restructured the sales team and reworked the strategy, and within a short period, they hit all their targets. Her performance impressed the top management at Bidvest, who expanded her sales role to cover five other businesses in the division. Brian Joffe heard of her accomplishments, and by May 2013 she found herself promoted to the board of directors of the Bidvest Group.

### Problem solver

'Handling sales is not easy, in any industry. But it's probably particularly hard when you can't differentiate your product, such as in the cleaning industry?' I wonder. 'What made you so successful in that role, coming from a background of economics and mathematics?'

'I think problem solving comes naturally to me,' explains Mpumi. 'That's why I was so good at maths – it's all about solving problems. Now, if you extrapolate that to sales, it's pretty much the same thing, because it's about working out what the customer value proposition is and working back in order to solve for it. We need to look at who the customer is, what they're trying to achieve and what their core strategy is. Only then can we immerse ourselves in the tendering process, because the solution we develop for, say, a banking group like ABSA will be different from the one we develop for a mining house such as Anglo American or a chemicals manufacturer such as Sasol.'

'Cleaning is cleaning – at the end, every customer just wants a hygienic building. But although the output is the same, how you get there is different for each client. One customer might be more focused on sustainability and you should therefore emphasise the environmentally friendly aspects of your products. Another customer might operate in an area where their interaction with the local community is important and you therefore need to demonstrate how the community will benefit from your services.'

After her appointment as executive director at the Bidvest group level, Mpumi extended these ideas, although she was less hands on when it came to pricing. Her position's title – Executive Director – was deliberately ambiguous, because she didn't want it to restrict the type of questions she could ask across different departments.

Mpumi spent more time looking for opportunities that cut across different divisions and sought to facilitate collaboration in the sales processes. The challenge was that Bidvest had seven different service lines (travel and hospitality; cleaning; freight; branded products; automotive; financial services; and commercial products). Often, they were submitting seven different bids for work and then ended up providing the customer with services that were not well coordinated. Her brief was to teach teams to think differently and align themselves in a manner that provides an integrated basket of seamless services to the customer.

Consequently, Bidvest ends up competing with itself, says Mpumi, because 'no other group can do everything we do in the way we do it'.

### Taking up the top spot

When Joffe first told Mpumi about his plans to make her the group CEO, she 'had a mini heart attack' she says. Years before, when she joined Prestige, she didn't even know that it was part of a massive conglomerate called Bidvest! Her ambitions didn't go beyond becoming the managing director of the cleaning company. That night when she got home, she told her husband that she didn't think Joffe was serious: a 37-year-old black woman is rarely in the conversation to lead a JSE-listed company. Besides, she thought, there were many more experienced and qualified people in the group who would be better suited to take up the post.

'I put the thought aside and decided to just focus on my work, because it can be dangerous walking around with the notion that you're the incoming CEO. I decided that nothing should change; I will continue to understand the business and deliver results. Having completed a master's degree in corporate finance a few years before, had also helped me to develop my skills further. Because mergers and acquisitions are part of our growth strategy, I needed to understand the fundamentals.'

After her appointment, Mpumi has continued to create cohesion in the teams and she's pleased that they're doing well. Yes, she admits, they've made mistakes along the way, but 'Bidvest's culture is to take responsibility for errors and fixing them quickly'.

'When the COVID pandemic hit, 75% of our services were classified as non-essential, meaning that a large part of our business halted operations,' Mpumi recalls. 'The Exco had a heated debate on how to deal with this and eventually resolved that we would have a "zero revenue, zero cost" approach in these businesses. On a spreadsheet, this meant that over 75 000 people would not receive a salary. We expected that the UIF (Unemployment Insurance Fund) would take care of them but when we realised that this would not be the case, we reversed the decision and set up a R400 million fund that ensured that everyone got paid.'

Bidvest was, however, forced to restructure to preserve liquidity, which meant closing down a number of branches in the ensuing un-predictable environment. Thankfully, Mpumi and her team have man-aged to bounce back after the pandemic to record strong results and recover lost jobs. The group has embraced her style of leadership, which differs sharply from that of previous Bidvest CEOs Brian Joffe and Lindsay Ralphs.

'For me, the X factor is values based leadership,' says Mpumi. 'Many CEOs are focused on delivering returns to shareholders. Bidvest employs over 120 000 people and in my view, we should focus first on creating value for them and our communities. If we manage to do that, we will undoubtedly create value for our shareholders. I'm also a firm believer in diversity, not just with regard to race but also when it comes to gender, skill and age. Corporate South Africa has a strong bias for employing finance people and chartered accountants; my approach is to employ people with different backgrounds. When you bring in people with diverse skill sets into your team, they bring in a different way of thinking, and ultimately your problem-solving capabilities will be a lot richer.'

### On work and life

The current Bidvest strategy was crafted in 2016 when the company unbundled its food service operations and listed it separately as Bid Corporation Limited (Bidcorp). This left Bidvest as an industrial entity and without an international footprint. The strategy set out what they wanted the company to look like, including what opportunities they would pursue locally and abroad as well as the capital allocation and gearing that they intended to have.

On taking over as CEO in October 2020, Mpumi did not have to re-set the strategy; her work was focused on accelerating its execution. Because of the earlier unbundling, which left Bidvest at less than half its original size, Mpumi feels like she's running an organisation that's just over six years old but with close to 40 years of experience. Having been in existence for so long gives the company the credibility in the market to execute its strategy despite a trimmed balance sheet.

'What makes our strategy a winning one is that it's simple and easy to understand,' Mpumi explains. 'It's also measurable, which means each divisional head can easily tell whether they're moving in the right direction. A strategy should clearly outline what success looks like, and to me success is about value creation. At the end of my time here, what I want to look back on is how this organisation changed people's lives, rather than how much profit we made.

'South Africa has significant structural challenges, which the government is struggling to get a grip on. The national leadership has failed to get even the most basic of things right and business has to step up and realise we cannot leave it to them. Gone are the days when corporate leaders shy away from things that were previously considered politics; we need to be involved in every way because that's the only way we can create value and provide a return to our shareholders.'

To Mpumi there's no such thing as work–life balance – the notion suggests that you can equalise work and life, she says, which she finds impossible.

'What I try to achieve is a work–life rhythm, so that I shift between work mode and family mode from time to time. I have just come back from six weeks' leave, during which I spent uninterrupted time with my family in December and a part of January. As the year begins, my rhythm changes and they now understand that I need to shift gears to focus on running this mammoth company again.'

Mpumi has two children: a 20-year-old daughter, Ipeleng, and a pre-teen son, Khumo. She enjoys playing board games with them and you can be guaranteed of a win in '30 seconds' if you're in Mpumi's team – as her long-time Michael Jackson anthem rang, you simply cannot beat her, she winks.

And when the board is packed up with the cards back in their boxes and everyone has turned in for the night, Mpumi likes to scroll through the offerings on Showmax and Netflix to binge on the latest shows. From 'the handsome Zulu boys on *The Wife*' to the feuding noble families on *Game of Thrones*, she always finds something to take her mind off the pressure that comes with having the weight of thousands of stakeholders on her shoulders.

# EDWARD KIESWETTER

*An obsession to serve*

'It is easy to stand on the sidelines and criticise. It is harder and
requires much more courage and dedication to roll up your sleeves,
step into the ring and help solve the problem.'

Edward Kieswetter, commissioner of the South African Revenue Services (SARS), is a fount of knowledge – natural intelligence combines with a wealth of long-earned learnings to culminate in solutions. Every question you ask him is met with an informed, well-considered reply, for which he chooses his words carefully. It's a joy to listen to him and I cannot help but think that during his time as a lecturer at the Cape Peninsula University of Technology (CPUT) and the Da Vinci Institute, his classes must have been packed.

I first met Edward in 2018 when the judges of the SA Professional Services Awards, an event I had conceptualised, conferred a Lifetime Achievement Award for excellence in management on him. Some years later he also appeared on the cover of an issue of my publication *The African Professional*.

'How is it that you ended up back at SARS?' I ask when we connect for our interview. Edward worked at SARS between 2004 and 2009, where he was the founding group executive of the Large Business Centre.

'I must have some sort of attraction to the public sector,' he responds with a warm, fatherly smile. 'I have a natural public service mindset. It's easy to stand on the sidelines and criticise those in government charged with service delivery. It's harder and requires much more

ALEXANDER FORBES, DA VINCI INSTITUTE & SARS's
**Edward Kieswetter**
*(Photo: Mzu Nhlabati)*

courage and dedication to roll up your sleeves, step into the ring and help solve the problem.

'SARS is a complex organisation and heading it is the same as heading a big corporation, regardless of the owner. Ultimately, you're answerable to stakeholders. In the case of SARS, the stakeholder is the government or, in the broader sense, South African citizens. When I was [group chief executive] at Alexander Forbes, I had to answer to shareholders. So, it's not different: you can't get away from being accountable.'

According to Edward, as the shareholders of SARS, South African citizens are much more vulnerable than the shareholders he served at a corporate such as Alexander Forbes. Their vulnerability stems from their not having the financial capital to exit as shareholders – it's only a very small proportion of the population who has the means to emigrate. Shareholders of listed companies can vote with their capital, but the citizenry is stuck with government institutions.

All the more reason why those who serve in public office should have an awareness of and respect for the fact that they hold in trust the life, the interest and the well-being of people who don't have a choice. 'I often think that public service – both at a political and at a bureaucratic level – lose sight of this. The whole state capture project was all about self-enrichment and self-interest. It was about the abuse of public office, not the use of public office to serve a higher cause.

'At least listed capital has no pretence about their aim, which is to create value for shareholders to whom they remain accountable. And if they don't deliver, those shareholders just toss them. Those in political office often get away with poor service delivery because the electorate do not have the same freedom and mobility. I would like to see a situation where those in public office are a lot more mindful of the higher purpose that calls us into service.'

For Edward, leadership is all about stewardship; there can be no better reason for someone to become a leader than to serve. He believes as a steward you should be driven by a burning desire to bequeath the next generation of leaders with a better organisation than what you had inherited. Of course, there's always some measure of self-interest in leadership, he muses, but you must subordinate your self-interest to the cause you serve and the organisation you lead.

It doesn't matter whether you're leading a tax authority, an educational institution or a financial services company, he says. Whether it is a public or private institution, as a leader your mandate is always to serve the common good.

### Tackling a turnaround with humility

Born in Maitland, Cape Town in 1958, Edward was one of five children. He had humble beginnings: as an eight-year-old boy he would go from door to door to help sell the clothes his seamstress mother had made.

After matriculating, he worked as a labourer at an engineering company in Cape Town and took evening classes at Athlone Technical College. Driven by a thirst for knowledge, he went on to obtain a National Diploma in Electrical Engineering (Peninsula Technikon, now CPUT), a Masters of Science in Education (University of the Western Cape), a Masters in Tax Law (North-West University) and a Masters of Business Administration (Henley Business School).

During his long career, Edward has worked for various organisations and in different roles, from an electronics and instrumentation engineer at Caltex Refinery to a lecturer at CPUT and later senior executive roles at Eskom and the FirstRand banking group. After five years at SARS, he joined Alexander Forbes Group Holdings, where he was part of the effort to turn around the company, which listed on the Johannesburg Stock Exchange soon after.

In 2016, Edward retired to run his personal portfolio of investments and took up the role of president and owner of a private university called the Da Vinci Institute. Three years into his 'retirement', he answered the call to help reform SARS. Edward had to resign from several roles, including that of lead independent director of Shoprite, board director of an international education company, and chairing the Da Vinci Institute board. Leaving these positions came at personal cost and he jokes that he should probably get his head checked for doing something few others would do.

'I came into a job I knew was going to be very difficult and one that, frankly, does not pay well. A recent article listed the top ten earners in government and my name was also there – but I was the only one the writer thought was underpaid! Fortunately, I'm in a phase of my life where money is not the primary driver. When I took the job, I was answering the call of *thuma mina* – to be part of the solution rather than to criticise from the sideline.'

On returning to SARS, Edward was saddened to see how an organisation that was admired by its international peers a decade ago had been severely weakened after becoming a victim of state capture.

'It was tragic for me to come back and to see the extent of the disrepair,' Edward laments. 'The reality is that no report, not even that of the Nugent Commission, could truly capture the real loss and damage that has come about. When I arrived, I looked into the eyes of people and I saw hurt. I listened to professionals who had been marginalised and bullied into submission. I saw the tears well up in their eyes as they told me their stories. It was then that I realised the truth that no report can fully reflect ...

'On top of that there was a loss of confidence by the public, a decline in the morale and the social fibre in the organisation. There was a decline in compliance levels, a proliferation of criminal activities and the subsequent decline in revenue performance. That was the situation I walked into in 2019.'

SARS has since managed to arrest these negative trends, he says. Their progress can be seen in improved revenue collection and the successful arrest and prosecution of perpetrators.

Edward and his team engineered this turnaround by doing a few important things. As a new leader, he walked in with humility because, as he says, 'one swallow does not make a summer'. He recognised that you can't stop state capture simply by appointing a new president or a new revenue commissioner; the entire system must change.

On his first day, Edward wrote a letter to his staff to introduce himself and to send a message that he unequivocally condemns state capture, since there were – and still are – some who deny that state capture took place. In the letter, he also explained what he believes he as the leader and they as the staff should hold each other accountable for.

His next step was to confront some of the widely publicised leadership challenges. Within the first few months, he instituted much-needed changes in the management composition of the organisation. He further provided an inspiring vision and strategic clarity by working with the top 70 leaders at SARS to craft a model that set out what was expected of the top structure. They cascaded this to the managers and staff signed an employee rights charter stating what every employee can expect from their manager.

'Although I think we have a great strategy, I don't believe it's what will win the war of transforming SARS. The engagement culture and leadership model are structured in a way that recognises that we will conquer the challenge by winning the hearts and minds of people. We've achieved a lot since 2019. But we cannot declare victory yet; we still have a long way to go.'

Some might find it surprising that Edward has been so successful in his turnaround strategy without getting help from a consulting firm. When I ask him about this, he says strategy formulation is a CEO's responsibility and that it doesn't make sense to outsource your thinking to someone else. To give strategic direction, hold leadership accountable and allocate resources are a leader's core competencies, which shouldn't be handed to others. Employing a third party to fulfil this role is like employing someone to teach your children values, he says.

His view is that you need consultants only in areas where you lack expertise and may take time to build capacity. SARS's project around cryptocurrency assets is a good example of where the organisation has indeed turned to third parties for help.

## *Six commandments*

I ask Edward what he thinks the X factor of corporate leadership is. He makes it clear that he doesn't believe in a silver bullet.

'I think it's situational … Some leaders are great at leading change, others at maintaining high performance. Then you get those who are good in structured bureaucracies and others do well in agile entre-preneurial cultures. I don't think there is a universal X factor that fits across all situations. I do think, however, that there's a common trend that every leader should exhibit, regardless of context.'

'And that is?' I prompt.

'Great leaders have a higher purpose. They also have two apparently paradoxical attributes. On the one hand, the fearless resolve to achieve something great; on the other, the genuine humility to acknowledge that they can't do it on their own. Good leaders genuinely seek to serve their stakeholders. They have an obsession to do the best they can for the people they purport to serve. I call that the "service obsession".

'Lastly, I think the greatest leaders invest in people. They are con-cerned about employees' growth and do not seek to merely extract their labour. It's an exchange: "You give me your time, your brilliance, your endeavour, and I give you the opportunity to become the best version of yourself, and, by the way, I also give you a pay cheque." These are the things that make up the universal essence of strong leadership.'

Edward goes on to say that a good strategy should tell a simple yet compelling story that inspires people. The simple test is that both an 85-year-old grandmother and a 10-year-old boy must be able to under-stand it. He cites the example of the biblical story of Moses who led the Israelites out of Egypt by telling them about the promise of a land of milk and honey in a way that made them excited about the future.

Like Moses, Edward has a set of commandments he lives by in his professional life. He calls them the six I's: intent, impact, inspiration, influence, insight and interdependency.

'Good leaders communicate strategic intent with clarity,' he starts to explain. 'They must have something they are prepared to die for – a passion they pursue with fearless resolve. There is nothing more soul destroying than having to follow a leader who either has no clear intent or is unable to communicate it clearly. I'm not referring to hollow rhetoric and platitudes, which we so often hear from leaders on soap boxes. It should be clear where we stand and what we stand for, what we wish to achieve, and whose interests we intend to serve.'

Edward warns that leaders should not stick mindlessly to their intent but should also consider the impact their decisions will have. 'A leader must have a heightened sense of mindfulness and concern. A steward leader always desires to have a positive impact and make a meaningful difference to people's lives,' he says.

Inspirational leaders, says Edward, are those who are able to connect with people at the highest or spiritual sense of who they are – the root of inspire is in fact 'in spirit'. They help people feel better about themselves and keep them hopeful, even when they despair. They keep a positive goal alive and rally their followers to excellence.

The fourth I is about having influence. Again, Edward turns to the example of the Israelites, who wanted to return to Egypt when they started doubting their journey to the New Land. 'A leader will not always have everyone's support, but you have to accept the responsibility to try and take everyone along, even those who may initially resist. Through positive example, demonstrable leadership and constant persuasion, steward leaders seek to influence the disbelievers, who often become their most ardent supporters in time.'

When talking about insight, Edward points out that employees might lose sight of an organisation's goal. 'When the journey becomes tough or when there's unforeseen adversity or a change in environment, even the willing followers may lose heart,' he says. 'Leaders must accept this and ensure that they themselves never become despondent. Instead, they should continually provide additional insight that will remove doubt, encourage recommitment and instil the belief that the goal is achievable.'

Lastly, bringing a group of people together to do a task does not automatically turn them into a high-performing team. Building such a team requires a conscious effort, Edward says. 'A steward leader helps people believe in their own abilities and appreciates the contributions of others. By embracing the diversity that each individual brings and getting others to value it too, the steward leader nurtures interdependence and builds a great team, where members look out for one another as they pursue individual and collective success. Central to this is how you create followership. There's no need for coercive or unethical tactics.'

Sticking to his six I's has served Edward well during his career. In 2022, *Daily Maverick* named him one of the People of the Year. Malibongwe Tyilo's pitch reads: 'Collecting tax is vital in South Africa because the fiscus supports a significant social welfare system – the largest in Africa and certainly one of the most significant in the developing world. To have accomplished what SARS has throughout COVID-19 (when the economy declined) and in a low-growth year, has been outstanding. Where it has been even more notable is retrieving the organisation from the jaws of capture and doing so without occupying the headlines.'

Despite his many accolades – which include SA Boss of the Year in 1999, ACO Dealmaker of the Year in 2015 and being a finalist in the All Africa Business Awards in 2016 – Edward remains humble. To him life is all about making small, positive differences to people in his personal, social and professional life. His greatest joy comes from knowing that he has been a blessing to others.

One can only imagine where South Africa could have been if there were more Edward Kieswetters leading our public institutions.

IMPERIAL & MOTUS's **Osman Arbee**
(Photo: Eunice Driver)

# OSMAN ARBEE

*The flexibility blueprint*

'You can be strict about your destination but not about your route.
Your vision must be flexible – within reason – because businesses,
economies and people change.'

'Colon cancer?'

Motus Group CEO Osman Arbee gasped as his doctor nodded. 'Well,
I guess it is what it is … What are my options?' he asked.

He had only one choice, his doctor said: immediate surgery. Five days
later, Osman was on the operating table, undergoing a procedure that
was meant to take six hours but lasted almost a full day. Although the
doctors managed to remove all traces of the tumour, Osman suffered
a stroke while he was in recovery, which left him partially paralysed
and unable to walk.

Back in the doctor's office after the operation, Osman demanded to
know what he could do to recover. The doctor recommended physio-
therapy and occupational therapy, and so started his journey back to
health.

When Graham Dempster, chairman of the Motus Group, visited him
at home, Osman told him the board should make a decision that would
be in the best interest of the business. 'If they think it's best for me
to retire early [from the position of CEO], I'm happy to go,' he told
Dempster.

His chairman replied that they'd give him six months to recover. If
he was unable to return by January the next year, then only would they
think about searching for a replacement.

Osman knew failure to recover was not an option. By October that year, four months after his surgery, there was hope. He was able to take a few steps and he could use his right hand again. A month later, he was driving – which was important, because he was getting depressed being cooped up all day. In December, he went on an overseas holiday, which did wonders to recharge him mentally.

'Initially I could only work for six hours, but over time I was able to get back to my usual 12 hours a day,' Osman tells me almost four years later. 'God has been very good to me. I am blessed because the cancer was removed, and it has not recurred – touch wood. I suffer from some side-effects of the stroke, but it's part of life. I've been able to lead this company successfully despite it all.'

### The accountant who wants to be close to the action

Osman grew up in a small town called Dullstroom in what is today's Mpumalanga. The closest Indian primary school was a boarding school in nearby Belfast and he matriculated from a boarding school in Standerton. Since he had been handling money from a young age at his father's general store, it was a natural choice to study accounting, for which he enrolled at the University of Durban Westville.

After graduating in 1982, he joined Deloitte Haskins & Sells in Johannesburg, one of the few big firms that employed people of colour during the apartheid years. He spent 23 years at the firm, rising to the position of audit partner and serving on the executive committee (Exco). He also singlehandedly got Deloitte appointed auditors of the Imperial Group.

In 2002, the United States Congress passed the Sarbanes–Oxley Act, a law governing financial record keeping. This impacted the audit profession as it was part of a body of regulations that limited the type of advice auditors could give clients. Osman was used to providing advice to owner-managed businesses – in fact, he was instrumental in getting companies such as Africa Glass Industries and Nandos listed on the stock exchange.

'Being an entrepreneur, giving business advice and understanding issues were in my blood. The accounting rules were not going to allow me to do that. And that's why I had to make a change. So I asked myself where I could use my skills best. The profession gave me a fantastic background, but I was looking for something different.'

Around that time, the top management of the Imperial Group called him to ask if he could assist with identifying a black chartered accountant to run their empowerment deals. He expressed an interest in the position himself, and despite them thinking he was overqualified for the job, they offered it to him in September 2004. In Osman's first 12 months at Imperial, he spent about R200 million on empowerment deals for the group.

He was deployed to the car rental and tourism division as CEO and was later appointed executive chairman of the motor retail division. Osman started an aftermarket automotive parts division, to supply parts for out-of-warranty vehicles, and bought the Midas business as part of that initiative.

In 2013, he was appointed chief financial officer of the Imperial Group, and promoted to Group CEO four years later. During the time of his cancer treatment, the strategy to unbundle the motor division and list it separately was afoot, and when he got back to the office in January, he came in as CEO of the separately listed Motus Group.

'I thank God I was fit enough to climb the stairs at the stock exchange and ring the bell,' Osman smiles. 'Soon after COVID-19 struck, our share price was at R28; today it's at about R120. We have a market capitalisation of R20 billion, which makes us the biggest motor group in the country, with operations in the UK, China, Taiwan and Australia. We now have our own identity – a separate building, a board of directors and an executive management team. All the members that were with me at the beginning are still here, and I think we've achieved something remarkable.'

### The entrepreneurial CEO

While Osman was at Imperial, the group imported cars for the retail and rental markets, but they did not deal in aftermarket parts. That meant they were not selling parts to cars that were outside the warranty period, and consequently as soon as a vehicle went out of warranty, they lost that business.

Initially the parts business did not do well, so Osman changed the strategy to make an acquisition. At the time, popular motor parts brand Midas was up for sale. 'I met with management, and they said a 25% share was available. I said, "No, that's not good enough. I need control." So, initially, we bought 60% and slowly purchased the rest of the shareholding. I had to buy a going concern, because starting a business unit from scratch was going to take too long and the school fees would be too high.'

After the success of the Midas acquisition, Motus also bought Alert Engine Parts and went on to add other businesses to that division too. Today they have about 30% market share, says Osman.

The company realised that acquisitions in the parts business was a good model and looked to understand it better. This led them to buying a parts wholesaler in Taiwan and also setting up a warehouse in Shanghai to store parts purchased in bulk in China before shipping to South Africa.

Motus explored further opportunities and found a small acquisition in the UK, which was bought for around R600 million (£30 million at the time). 'Through this business we understood the mechanics, the market, procurement and margins. We believed we now knew enough to buy another business and recently purchased a bigger operation in the UK for R3.7 billion.'

According to Osman, having the aftermarket parts business has removed the cyclical nature of dealing only in new cars and pre-owned cars. He explains that because they had to create some stability for their shareholders with regard to returns, they expanded the aftermarket parts business as it ensures a balance between South African and foreign income.

'Our target is to get about 24% foreign income and 25% profit out of the aftermarket parts business in 2023. We also have the mobility solutions business, which is not dependent on new car sales and so provides added stability. I have balanced my portfolio between cyclical and non-cyclical, South African and non-South African, to give us stability.'

## Understanding cycles

In South Africa about 550 000 vehicles are sold a year, but during the global financial crisis of 2008, the figure dropped to about 350 000. Banks stopped funding customers and it took two years to get out of that cycle. After a few years things improved, but then COVID hit, and car sales dropped to 386 000 vehicles. In 2022, new car sales were on track to reach 520 000 again. In this business, says Osman, you should therefore expect to hit a bump after two or three years of good sales.

When new car sales are down, it means people are driving older cars that need service outside of warranty – which is why the aftermarket parts business makes so much sense. South Africa has 12 million cars on the road (including the taxi market), with only a little more than a quarter under warranty.

In the UK, there are 40 million vehicles on the road and the proportion of cars outside of warranty is similar, meaning about 30 million cars need aftermarket parts. The sheer size of the market is what attracts Osman. It may be competitive, but with procurement channels established in the Far East and now also Turkey, he believes they can get reasonable market share in the next 18 months.

Up to now, Motus has not ventured into the rest of the continent, for a number of reasons. Firstly, cars flood dirt cheap into Africa from places such as Hong Kong, Dubai, Japan and Singapore. As a result of the competition from these 'grey imports' (new or used cars that move legally from one country to another, but through a different distribution system than that of the car manufacturer), the new car market in Africa is very small, Osman explains.

'There's no consistency in the types of vehicle being sold, so you can't be sure which spare part will sell,' he says. 'You may carry a certain type of spark plug and later discover you have too much of the wrong thing because you don't have the history of the vehicles.

'The market is very informal. For example, in Lagos you'll find a part store, with a workshop then right in front. There's no infrastructure and it's difficult to get information on which vehicles are being sold. It's because the range of parts needed is too big that we've stayed away.'

Osman also points out that parts are generally not bought in bulk in the rest of the continent; in most of the African markets people buy parts on a daily basis. In addition, he says, you have to be realistic: if someone buys a 10-year-old car, they're not going to get a new premium spark plug, but will likely settle for a cheap second-hand one.

### A flexible vision

Osman advises leaders to surround themselves with intelligent people whom they trust and share a vision with. If you're hungry enough to achieve what you set out to do, nothing will stop you. If everyone on the team agrees on the vision, everyone will be committed to it, he believes. But, he warns, it's easy to talk in the boardroom; it's much harder to do it in practice. If CEOs aren't dedicated to their company's vision, they will end up doing things that are counterproductive, which will eventually lead to failure because you cannot micromanage all your businesses.

'A vision is like a journey', says Osman. 'If you're travelling from Johannesburg to Cape Town, it doesn't matter whether you go via Bloemfontein or Kimberly, the vision remains the same – to get to Cape Town.

'You can be strict about your destination but not about your route, because that would make you an entrepreneur with tunnel vision. Your vision must be flexible – within reason – because businesses, economies and people change. It's not an easy skill; it's something that you develop over time with your team.'

Motus demonstrated great flexibility when the COVID-19 pandemic struck. They had a rental car fleet of 25 000 vehicles, which they intended to grow but instead had to bring down to 8 000 during 2020. The rental cars were an illiquid asset and they needed cash, so Osman instructed the team to sell them over an eight-month period. They decided to take their time because he did not what to flood the market and damage residual values.

The cash generated from these sales, freezing capital expenditure and retrenching some staff brought the group's debt down from R9 billion to R4 billion. Now that the immediate crisis is over, they're building up the fleet again and expect to be back at 25 000 vehicles by the end of 2023.

At Motus, doing business in an ethical way is engrained through having good governance principles in place. They run regular internal audits in the company and the legal department ensures that processes are robust. Staff are required to trade in a fair and reasonable way, never overpromising and then under-delivering. Integrity issues are minimised because the bulk of profits come from new car sales. The 65 used-car dealerships in the group sell cars from the rental business that are between 9 and 15 months old and have a detailed service history.

'If you buy a car from me and I do a bad deal, that is the last time I will see you because you won't come back to me to service your car. That will be a terrible outcome, because I actually do not make real money on selling the car; it's the servicing that is profitable.

'When we take trade-ins of cars that are over five years old and have high mileage, we sell them to traders, because those cars are often problem children. You sell it to a customer today and tomorrow the aircon is not working. The customer will blame you, even though it is just an old car with no functional guarantees.'

### The power of positivity

Osman's health setbacks have shown him the benefits of positive thinking. 'You cannot get depressed with these things, because whatever is meant for you is meant for you. I can't change it and you can't change it, and the doctors can only do their best. A positive mindset and great support from my wife and family helped me a lot. I was also thankful to my colleagues for not pressuring me and being willing to keep my job for me for six months.'

Osman tries to forget negative things that happen in a work context and rather focus on the positive. In managing people, he says it's key to never play the person – because then you end up with an enemy. If you deal with the issue, the focus shifts away from the people and you will get the right result for the business. If you make things personal, you are likely to come up with the wrong business answer.

'It's a philosophy I have maintained over the years: deal with issues and let people be part of a process. Of course, sometimes you have no option. For example, if you have to deal with a person who is a racist: their racism is an inherent characteristic of their personality and it does not fit with the organisation. I can usually separate the problem from the personal, but when a person is part of the problem, I must deal with them.'

At close to 65, Osman says he's ready for a mental break from the events of the last difficult five years and that he is considering retiring. Not that one expects him to be away from the grind for too long, for positive and experienced entrepreneurs like Osman will always have a home in South African business.

CAPITEC BANK

# GERRIE FOURIE

*The simplicity specialist*

'My passion was always to be an entrepreneur and build something ...
It is the entrepreneurial spirit that actually attracts me, not so much the CEO role.'

'It's not rocket science' people say when something is easy to do or understand. In *Simplicity for Success in Business*, Peter Eckart, rocket scientist who turned management consultant, writes that people generally prefer simplicity: when you buy a new cell phone, car or any other device, you don't want to read a lengthy manual before you can use the thing.

It's not different in business, his argument goes, and businesses that simplify life for their consumers will have an advantage over those that don't.

Capitec has seen this first hand. Ranked the world's best bank in 2018 by the respected Lafferty Group's Global Bank Quality benchmarking study, they attribute their success to mastering simplicity. 'When you do something in a simple and transparent manner, the client understands it and has a measure of control,' CEO and co-founder Gerrie Fourie tells me.

But it doesn't mean achieving simplicity is easy. Eckart paraphrases Albert Einstein when he writes that 'simplicity is 1% talent and 99% hard work'. Simply put, making things simple is hard work.

To be successful, you must differentiate your product from the market, and if it is not differentiated, you have to perform 20%–30% better than your competitors, Gerrie explains. This requires a strong culture of innovation and thinking differently.

CAPITEC BANK's **Gerrie Fourie**
*(Photo: Courtesy of Capitec)*

A strategy based on simplicity is easy to define, but its success sits in the execution. Yet if everyone in the organisation understands it, it becomes easy to implement. So, in the banking world, Gerrie says, when a client walks into a bank, they expect customer service. Getting customers to walk out satisfied with the service, is the ultimate test of whether the strategy is working.

'We have about 10 000 consultants, and if we design a product, we must ensure that they all understand it exactly the same way. If there's variation in their understanding, it causes confusion – and ultimately client dissatisfaction. We therefore strive to invest not only in simplicity of design but also in how we train our people to understand both our strategy and our systems.

'The way we set up our branches is such that both the client and the consultant see the same screen; as a result, there's no room for confusion.'

The Capitec model treats all customers exactly the same; it doesn't matter whether you're rich or poor. So everyone gets a black card (no different colours for different income levels, as at some other banks) and the fee structure is the same for all customers. The service is also similar because products are uniform, making it easy for consultants to understand and sell their offerings.

## An entrepreneurial drive

A Free State boy at heart, Gerrie attended Grey College in Bloemfontein, from where he matriculated in 1981. He then moved south to obtain a BCom degree, followed by an honours in accounting, both from Stellenbosch University.

Gerrie learnt a lot about business from his entrepreneur father, who never worked for a salary or for somebody else. As a young boy he would spend Friday afternoons and weekends with his dad installing telephone poles across the Free State. Working with his dad taught him not only about the value of hard work, but also to think innovatively to solve problems.

Gerrie started his career in the financial planning division at Stellenbosch Farmers' Winery, where he managed the winery's sales and distribution for five years. At 27 he was appointed manager of the then Natal division of the company, a position for which the MBA he completed through his alma mater a few years earlier prepared him well.

His master's studies made him rethink how the business should be run. 'At the time, it was standard practice for restaurants to wait 48 hours to get a delivery and I led the change towards same-day deliveries. Probably the biggest value in the course was group discussions about case studies. People from different industries offered different views, and our discussions around suitable strategies were intense.'

Although Gerrie believes young professionals can benefit from doing an MBA, he cautions about pursuing the qualification just for the sake of it. 'When considering further studies, think carefully about whether you want to go into management or if you'd be better off specialising in your field of expertise,' he advises.

He didn't have a specific ambition to become a corporate executive, he tells me. 'My passion was always to be an entrepreneur and to build something. So, when Michiel le Roux contacted me with the idea to start a bank, I jumped at the opportunity because it promised to fulfil that desire. Even after all these years, I don't see my function as only being a CEO, but rather as being part of building an organisation.

'We have exciting plans for business banking, beyond our retail offering, and it's this entrepreneurial approach that attracts me, not so much the CEO role.'

### A bank in your pocket

Gerrie is immensely proud of the success of their simplicity mantra, which has attracted 19 million clients and led to the opening of 850 branches of the bank. He says many people come up with great ideas, but then fail to put it on paper as a proper business plan.

'I remember when we started the bank, we spent about nine months writing that business plan and there was much debate on what we were going to do. We eventually agreed that we'll focus on affordability, accessibility, simplicity and service. These have been our four fundamentals since the start and we execute on it in everything we do still today.'

There will always be political events, economic shifts and other curveballs along the way that call for management to be agile to achieve set goals. But the fundamentals and the founders' vision remain unchanged.

'Capitec was built for low-income customers,' Gerrie says. 'Our service became so good that we have attracted higher-income earners to the extent that we now have 16–18% market share in that bracket. With 35–40% of the lower-income category banking with us, we now have 19 million active clients, which makes us the biggest bank on customer volume. Importantly, more than half our customers are using our digital platforms, which assists us greatly in practising our four fundamentals. Having digital access means that you have the bank in your pocket 24 hours a day.'

To Gerrie, leadership is about ensuring that everyone understands the 'why' and the 'what' questions someone can ask about the company. Why does the company exist? What is its objective? Part of this is effective communication, which often means that explaining something only once is not enough. Gerrie believes the leadership team should constantly repeat the company's vision, objectives and strategy for it to be properly understood and reinforced.

'You cannot be complacent; no company is too big to fail,' he cautions. 'We remember times when everyone had a Kodak camera and a Nokia phone. These were once massive companies, but today they're mere shadows of their past. Our culture in the bank is based on enhancing client experience while keeping staff motivated. If you challenge yourself all the time to deliver on client needs, you're unlikely to fail. Understanding client needs requires humility and agility.'

### Facing challenges head on

Gerrie's counsel to any upcoming professional is to understand what drives you. If you want to play the guitar, then strum those strings on a grand scale!

'When I was 24, I asked my CEO Dave Marlow for advice,' he reminisces. 'He said that a career has three stages. When you first go into a job, you are trying to understand the job, making certain you know the A to Z of it. The next phase is to put your stamp of approval on it, making the job your own. In the third stage, you progress to developing a colleague and then move on. The last stage is probably the most challenging because people underestimate it, but it is actually the mark of true leadership.'

Gerrie also recommends not being afraid to question things and to ask when you don't understand something. And to ask again, if it remains unclear. 'Keep at it until you understand how everything fits together. People very quickly think they know what's happening, even when they don't really,' he says. 'At a leadership level, you must explain to people why they have to do something because when they understand why things are done the way they are, people will also know what is expected of them.'

Banking will likely change in the future to encompass financial services that are about more than just saving, reckons Gerrie. What will be critical, is the availability of data and how you optimise its use for value add and customer satisfaction.

Banks will also have to think about how cryptocurrency and blockchain technology are going to influence the way they do business in the future. According to Gerrie, institutions that think of the end-to-end client experience, instead of the experience a client derives from a single product will come out at the top.

The Capitec group recently purchased Mercantile Bank and have also obtained an insurance licence. These two developments offer opportunities to expand the business. I ask Gerrie whether acquiring Mercantile, a business bank, does not conflict with their orginal focus of servicing the lower-income bracket.

'Not at all,' he says. 'There are many small and medium enterprises with banking needs and business banking is complex. We intend to use the same model we have for retail banking by simplifying the opaque arena of business banking. South Africa needs thriving small businesses to achieve real growth and development.'

As we conclude, I offer to pen Gerrie's biography when he eventually downs his tools in a few years. But he declines with a humble chuckle, saying he will be too busy coaching young entrepreneurs to make time for a book about himself.

True to his company's philosophy, even in retirement, he'll hanker after simplicity and service.

BARLOWORLD & LETSEMA's **Isaac Shongwe**
*(Photo: Mzu Nhlabati)*

# ISAAC SHONGWE

### The giver CEO

> 'I am not in business simply to buy and sell and make
> a profit. I approach business from a different angle:
> I see it simply as a catalyst for social good.'

Organisational psychologist Adam Grant contends that how one inter-acts with others is a predictor of one's success. In his book *Give and Take*, he describes three kinds of people. A taker is someone who tries to get as much from others as they can, asking only 'what can you do for me?' A matcher is someone with a *quid pro quo* mentality – 'I will do something for you, but only if you do something for me'. But givers are the people who contribute to others without expecting anything in return. They are always thinking about what they can do to help others.

And in this system, founder of Letsema and former CEO of Barlo-world, Isaac Shongwe, is a giver – one of only about 25% of people, according to Grant.

Although some givers get exploited and burn out, the rest achieve extraordinary results across a wide range of industries. Studies show that a culture of helping and mentoring others lets organisations per-form better in every metric – customer satisfaction, profitability, employee retention and operating expenses. In contrast, takers, who make up about 19% of people, rise and fall quickly, their progress being halted by the 55% or so of people who are matchers.

Isaac Shongwe is indeed a classic giver. I met him in 2016 when I was enlisted for the Africa Leadership Initiative Media Fellowship. The fellowship is Isaac's brainchild, a project he founded as part of his participation in the Aspen Global Leadership Network. Through Isaac's sponsorship and the support of Bloomberg, the costly programme has hosted tens of young Africans in several locations, from Kigali to New York, for in-depth discussions on how to uplift the continent.

I am delighted that Isaac agreed to speak to me and during our interview he revealed things that few probably know about him, including that he is dyslexic. He's had to work really hard to overcome the learning disorder that made it difficult for him to read complicated words or write well. But he developed a workaround for himself where he breaks down words into two or three simpler parts to understand or write them.

Linked to this condition, Isaac also used to stutter, which made him a target for bullies during his school years. Frustrated by the ridicule, he would lash out and fight. 'Over time I came to understand that aggravating a situation does not solve anything,' Isaac says wisely today. 'The experience taught me to handle conflict in both personal and professional situations.

'I often get up and walk away from unhealthy situations. It's pointless to engage with those who have ill intentions or to develop relationships that are not beneficial. Because of my dyslexia, I also learnt to prepare thoroughly for any engagement to ensure seamless delivery. Before any meeting, I repeatedly go over all the salient points.'

### The early years

Isaac traces his business prowess to watching his grandmother selling handmade Ndebele beads on credit. As a boy, he was part of making sales and collecting debts. His grandmother used the money to educate her grandchildren, and this made Isaac ponder how he could help. He decided to buy and sell apples in the village and as demand soared, he recruited four of his friends to help with distribution.

He completed high school in South Africa in the early 1980s and his good grades earned him a scholarship to do his A levels in the UK. He then proceeded to the US for tertiary studies at Wesleyan University. He remembers the first time he visited New York City, walking down

Wall Street, completely in awe of the tall buildings American capitalists had built. His curiosity about their triumphs led him to find out more about the rise of trade in the West and in so doing he learnt about the nexus between business and politics.

Isaac's interactions with the ANC branch in New York convinced him that South Africa would need good businesspeople to foster change when freedom eventually came. As a result, he switched his major from politics in his first year to a double major incorporating economics as a sophomore. After graduating, he returned to South Africa, in 1987, with the goal of going into business to accelerate change.

Even though he is a good businessman, Isaac says he has a love–hate relationship with business; his gift is also his curse. 'There are many people who enjoy being involved in buying and selling and making a profit, but I am not one of them. I approach business from a different angle: I see it simply as a catalyst for social good. My interests are in doing things for others and in nation building.'

Isaac's scepticism about business is largely due to his growing up in the apartheid era. He believes that, like slave owners and colonialists, apartheid capitalists were driven by greed without due regard for corporate social responsibility.

Isaac started his career in 1988 when Barloworld employed him as a management trainee. A year later he was selected as the second black South African Rhodes scholar to pursue an MBA at Oxford University. The company continued to pay 40% of his salary, which enabled him to complete the house he was building for his grandmother. The company also kept his job for him and on his return, he was given more responsibilities. This was the foundation for eventually starting his own business, Letsema Consulting, in 1996.

### Partnerships: the good, the bad and the downright ugly

At Letsema's inception, Isaac went into partnership with others. However, misalignment with his partners eventually destroyed the organisation five years in, and he had to go back to the starting point to reconfigure the business. His partner today was his third employee, Derek Thomas.

'Figuratively speaking, Derek and I went to war together and that helped us gain a deeper understanding of each other. The partnership is well defined between ownership and reporting hierarchy. This is particularly important for an entrepreneur who is starting a company, more so than it is for big corporates. In larger entities, it is somewhat easier to form partnerships because the relationship is quite specific and the roles to be played are outlined from the outset.

'Business partnerships can be very hard,' Isaac says. 'We know things can become difficult in a marriage. The same can happen in business. It requires alignment on both sides, as well as an awareness of both yourself and your partner. Before engaging in a partnership, you should be very clear about what you're looking for. People make the mistake of taking a partnership lightly because the partner is bringing money or a lucrative opportunity into the business. They engage others without fully understanding the person and then they realise only down the line that they are misaligned when it comes to strategy and values.'

Isaac learnt this painful lesson through many partnerships over the years. One that haunts him to this day is his seat on the board of New Africa Investments Ltd, which taught him valuable lessons about engaging with unions. He decided to enter that space and approached the Chemical, Energy, Paper, Printing, Wood and Allied Workers' Union (CEPPWAWU) for a partnership through which they formed an investment company with a profit split of 70% to the union and 30% to Letsema. One of the deals Isaac secured for the partnership was with Aspen Pharmacare in 2001 and subsequently het set up similar ventures with Sasol and Nampak.

'After the change in leadership in the ANC in 2008, there was a shake-up in the CEPPWAWU hierarchy. The new union leaders contested the arrangement I had with them, resulting in a long, expensive court battle. The lesson I learnt from that experience was that I should have set up a shareholding structure in which I had actual equity rather than having a profit-sharing arrangement that was subject to challenge. I would advise entrepreneurs to think hard about the mechanisms they put in place when forming partnerships to protect their interests, in case the actors in the arrangement change.'

Entrepreneurs often feel they have to move with speed to exploit opportunities and end up partnering too quickly. He repeatedly likens it to a smitten youngster wanting to get married. Take the time to get to know your partner before you walk down the aisle, he cautions. And even if you know your partner well, know that it will take hard work to get the marriage right.

Today Isaac is very strategic in his outlook and extremely focused. An important attribute of a leader, or any professional for that matter, he says, is having self-awareness: knowing your strengths and weaknesses. He's good at reading people and building relationships with the right individuals. On a one-hour flight, for example, he can easily strike up a conversation with a fellow passenger and by the time they disembark, he would know whether that person has a business opportunity worth pursuing.

While he is a good hunter who always sees the big picture, he admits that he lacks attention to detail. But this is one of Thomas's strengths. And it's this counterbalance that contributes so much to Letsema's success: Isaac brings in the opportunities and Derek handles the execution.

### Barloworld and black economic empowerment

Another catastrophic partnership was in DNA Supply Chain Investments, a company Isaac and three other entrepreneurs set up in 2001. Isaac essentially took a profitable logistics contract he had with Spoornet into the partnership. The company grew quickly and listed on the Johannesburg Stock Exchange just months after it was formed.

But feuding founding partners led to the company's liquidation in 2003. With the experience he had gained in logistics, Isaac approached Barloworld with a proposal to be their black partner. They provided him with the requisite guarantees to get funding for a 26% stake in Barloworld Logistics.

'In 2005, I left Derek to run Letsema and took up the role of executive in charge of business development at Barloworld Logistics,' recalls Isaac. 'I was promoted to CEO a year later. Initially I only wanted to work there for five years, but the 2008 global financial crisis interrupted my plans, leading to my stay extending to 2013. We built a high-growth company and the contracts I put in place are still there. The money I made from selling my shares when I exited gave me a reasonable balance sheet to do other deals. Consequently, Letsema now has several controlling stakes in profitable businesses.'

While his involvement in Barloworld had a lot to do with the policy of black economic empowerment (BEE), Isaac believes the scheme has been very bad for black entrepreneurship.

'Many people do not like it when I say that, but it's the truth. You cannot legislate behaviour. BEE is a distributive model that says that because of the sins of the past, companies need to give out 25% of their businesses. But we're not creating mechanisms and systems that build black businesses. It has been 28 years since democracy, and you will struggle to identify a black business that was built from scratch and became a colossal enterprise.'

Isaac points out that there are many individuals who have made a lot of money 'but have not built a thing' – and that is why he has an obsession to build something at Letsema that will outlive him. 'Sadly, it is easier to cite big black companies that have failed than those that have succeeded. There are some BEE billionaires who own stakes in companies that are quite white at their core.

'The executive leadership of these companies come from the old order and the black owners are not actively trying to cultivate black excellence. Although we may criticise a country such as Nigeria for ills like corruption, the big companies there – banks, telecommunication entities and schools – are owned by Nigerians who built them from the ground up.'

## *Letsema Foundation*

Isaac has always believed that doing things right in business will give you the resources, leverage and power to pursue the things you really care about. The foundation he set up at Letsema has given him the platform to do so. 'It's not been easy but thankfully I've been mentored by people with a philanthropic mindset, such as George Soros, who I met as chairman of the Open Foundation for South Africa,' Isaac says.

'Letsema now annually gives a lot to causes that I care about. Business must play a fundamental part in society, but instead, it is unfortunately often abused to oppress others. We have a pyramid where close to half of the world's wealth is owned by 1% of the global population and a vast majority wallow in abject poverty.

'I built the Letsema business to be like a family. We don't all look the same, but if one does well, one is rewarded well. I think we have built a decent business, which allows me to do the things I need to do. As a key sponsor of the Africa Leadership Initiative, Letsema enabled the creation of a fellowship of individuals from government, business and the civil society who are committed to promoting value-based leadership on the continent. Lately, we have pioneered the Young African Leadership Initiative, which is aimed at grooming Africans under the age of 35 to be co-creators of a good society.'

Isaac observes that most people set out to go into business with no other goal than to make lots of money. However, money does not necessarily make them better or happier people.

'How much land is enough? At some point you should realise that you should use the resources amassed to make the world a better place. I am grateful that my success in business allows me to spend 70% of my time on non-business activities, such as chairing the Wits University Council where I am critical to the institution's strategy. I feel I have a duty to contribute to the education sector because others paid for my education. Consequently, Letsema Foundation pays the fees of many children from previously disadvantaged backgrounds.'

Continued engagement in activities that make society a better place attracts even more business, because this leads to the development of relationships based on the right values. According to Isaac, Letsema currently has more deal flow than they can cope with because people want to do business with individuals they feel they can trust. 'What is the determining factor on who to engage with?' I ask.

'It's whether they have an ethical backbone.'

### Crafting successful strategies

A strategist par excellence, Isaac explains that while strategies must be well thought out, they need not be complicated. During the times he lived in the UK and US, he was a good striker on the soccer field and captained most of the teams he played for. His involvement in soccer informs his views on strategy: if you want to win, you must go into the game with a plan. This includes identifying gaps and exploiting them.

In this regard, Isaac admires a business such as Capitec, whose founders identified a need and thought about what solutions they could develop to address it. They mobilised resources and established the right distribution channels to provide a financial institution for the millions of black South Africans without bank accounts. They studied how to make it easier and 20 years later they're overtaking institutions that are decades older.

'I think the Afrikaner businessmen have pivoted better than their English counterparts,' Isaac states. 'Curro [a group of private schools] is another example. A few Afrikaner educators identified the need to provide black children with quality private education. They are proof that you do not need the complicated matrices and fancy Power-point presentations you get from consulting firms to have a success-ful strategy.

'I've seen this in our own business, too. Letsema invested in a busi-ness in the [KwaZulu-Natal] Midlands that owns 25 000 hectares of forest and produces trusses for the building industry. Among the trees they discovered a water source and started to develop a bottling plant for spring water. Today that business is growing at over 30% per annum and they supply Woolworths with their in-house water brand and the Thirsti brand,' he says.

The trailblazer who was forced into the world of business by his enterprising grandmother has taken the business ball and run with it. Like the soccer fans who cheered him from the sidelines, fellow South Africans are rooting for Isaac Shongwe to reach even greater heights as he 'uses business as a catalyst for social change'.

MOMENTUM METROPOLITAN HOLDINGS' **Jeanette Marais**
*(Photo: Pieter du Toit)*

# JEANETTE MARAIS

*Setting standards, selling dreams*

'Having everyone on a team know their targets and what they need to
do every day, every week and every month can have a big impact – it can
turn around an organisation.'

Born in the Free State in 1967, today's deputy CEO at Momentum
Metropolitan Holdings and CEO: Momentum Investments, Jeanette
Marais, was raised in a farming family and had a fairly ordinary childhood. When she graduated in 1989 with a major in mathematical studies from the then University of the Orange Free State, she did not get
much career guidance about what she could do with her degree. It was
when she started her actuarial studies at the Faculty of Actuaries in
Scotland, that she was advised to get work experience if she wanted
to qualify as an actuary.

'With my quiet Afrikaans upbringing, I never foresaw this career,'
Jeanette says with a soft yet authoritative voice. 'As a young girl,
I thought to myself that I was somewhat clever and that I would get a
degree, work, meet someone, marry and have kids. But I cannot say
that I had this driving ambition to become a CEO.

'When people ask me how I got to the top, I say it's not like I knew
what elevator to pick. When I take stock, a lot of it is pure luck and
being at the right place at the right time.'

A professor at the University of Pretoria helped her to get a job at
Momentum, which at the time was still a much smaller company, Jeanette says. She spent the first 10 years of her career in the actuarial
and then sales and marketing departments at the company before being
headhunted by PSG. Interestingly, she has never had to compile a CV

for job-hunting purposes; every job that she's had since had been offered to her.

She recalls a pivotal moment at Momentum when her team came up with the idea to launch an investment platform. They created a transparent flexible product that was so radical that management asked four of them to sit in a room and build it from within because they saw the opportunity it presented. That experience shaped her career in investment and distribution.

Despite excelling in her actuarial science studies, Jeanette felt she could do so much more than spreadsheets and sums. The more she studied the technical information, the less involved she became with people in the organisation. She decided to rather use the knowledge she had accumulated to do something else. At that stage she was well positioned to be the bridge between the front and back offices.

The marketing and distribution people would express the need for a product; she would explain it to the actuaries in a way that they understood. 'Before, actuaries would build something and present it with a "Ta-daa!", only for the marketing people to moan that the product was not what they had asked for. Playing the role of translator between the departments set me up at the heart of Momentum to assist both products and clients.

'With every product that was developed, I could ask pertinent questions about whether it was right for our clients and if it was ready to go to market. That kind of client obsession is something that has driven me throughout my career.'

### The key to a high-performance culture

In January 2003, Jeanette was appointed director of distribution at STANLIB. The role was to distribute STANLIB's products through advisers. As part of her responsibilities, Jeanette was asked to lead the merger between Standard Bank and Liberty Asset Management.

It was no easy task; these were two completely different businesses, with divergent cultures. The management skills she needed to oversee such a marriage were quite different from those she needed at Momentum and PSG.

When the merger was complete, she decided to move on because she was living in Cape Town and the job required her to commute to Johannesburg each week. In 2005, she joined Old Mutual and was charged with starting a specialist investment business. The company felt it was failing with high-net-worth advisors and clients, and they wanted Jeanette to start a unit that could focus on that area of the market. After nine months they asked her to become the head of Broker Distribution.

Jeanette's role was to turn around a business that was making terrible losses and was looking to break even. She was given five years and was not allowed to hire additional employees because they had to keep the cost base down. In fact, they wanted Jeanette to retrench people, but she protested against such an action and argued that there were better ways of reducing costs. She convinced the company that they could improve the situation by creating a high-performance culture.

'I got every team member to know their targets and what they needed to do every day, every week and every month. Those few small things have a big impact – it can turn around and lead an organisation in a completely different direction. In three years, the business turned a profit.'

Jeanette was at Old Mutual for five years before Allan Gray approached her to co-head their retail business. She explains that few people would say 'no' to the respected Allan Gray brand. In fact, she thought that it would be her last job, because she viewed Allan Gray as the ultimate investment company in South Africa.

Leaving the company 10 years later as an executive director was one of her toughest career decisions. 'After much thought, I figured that a decade at Allan Gray was more than enough for me in the sense that it was already doing well as a business when I got there. I can proudly say I took it to new heights in terms of its retail business by fostering an obsession with client service.

'After completing an MBA through the International Institute for Management Development (IMD) in Switzerland, I came back with the belief that I could bring about change and make things bigger. However, Allan Gray is a family business that is privately owned, which means it didn't have the appetite for drastic changes. I felt like I was in a comfort zone and I didn't feel challenged or excited. I have friends who thought I was crazy for leaving such a comfortable position. I could hang around and take expensive holidays, but that is just not me.'

Every role in which Jeanette had the opportunity to truly grow a business has been memorable for her. Another example is the investment platform at Allan Gray that was the sixth largest in the country when she joined, but the biggest when she left. To take things to new heights with the STANLIB merger and to turn around the Old Mutual business are other highlights.

'There is always a bar that can be raised because by the time you've reached one goal, you need to figure out what the next one is. It is hard to pinpoint low points because you make mistakes everywhere, but even those are learning opportunities. Nothing has ever stopped me dead in my tracks or had the potential to destroy my career. There would be disappointment sometimes, for sure, like positions I thought I'd get but didn't. But that's life. You miss the elevator, so you take the stairs and get to the desired landing.

'My husband always says, "Sheesh, Jeanette, you are such a positive person: everywhere you work you claim is the best place, the best company, the best job!" I simply make the best out of every situation.'

### Insisting on high standards

One day a non-executive board member, who was in a senior position when Jeanette worked at Momentum, called her to say that they desperately needed her expertise. At the time the group was struggling and several fundamentals were wrong. The negotiations for her return took nine months, and three things were deciding factors in her decision.

Firstly, she felt that she needed a challenge and the task to turn around the company promised just that. Jeanette loves the idea of taking a struggling business and giving people hope again, to see the flame ignited in employees' eyes again.

Secondly, Hillie Meyer, Jeanette's first boss at Momentum, was asked to return as group CEO. Jeanette would be his deputy. She had stayed in touch with Hillie over the years and knew they would have a good working relationship, which could lead Momentum through the much-needed changes.

'The third reason is that ever since I left Momentum, it was the one company I never liked beating. Every time we won something over Momentum, I was a bit sad and sometimes I would have preferred to let one go to them. I've always had a deep love and admiration for the company. It was enticing to think I could help rewrite its story.'

Jeanette rejoined Momentum in March 2018 and today her job is bigger than her role at Allan Gray. The portfolio of businesses that report to her is large and complex – she heads distribution and is also a connector of that business to the investment company. Jeanette loves that when Momentum builds a product, they ask how it connects to clients.

She has won many fans in her efforts to rebuild Momentum. 'Jeanette is someone who really sees the potential or the dream and conveys it to her teams,' says Michelle van der Watt, an executive associate. 'She is a leader who really lights a fire in you. She puts people first and helps them to fulfil their potential and goals. She takes businesses to new heights.'

Anneke Hanekom, head of reputation management, agrees. 'Jeanette is a hard task master with really high standards ... I will not pitch up at a meeting with anything substandard because she will not mince her words. But I've also gone to Jeanette at times when I felt very vulnerable and uncertain, because she is emotionally trustworthy ... and we would work through it together.'

Other people who have worked with Jeanette have called her 'fundamentally unreasonable' as far as standards are concerned. This probably stems from her father's approach when she was growing up. When Jeanette came home having achieved 98% in maths and being top of her class, he would ask her why she was celebrating 98% when she knows she could achieve 100%.

This is how she carries herself, in and outside whatever organisation she works for and even those she's not involved with! For instance, at the end of a flight, she is the type of person who would send feedback to the airline with tips on how they could improve their service.

At Momentum Metropolitan, she hopes to be the kind of leader employees would come to when there is a crisis. She says she is happy to back staff members as long as they do not come with nasty surprises. At the first sign of trouble, she wants to know what is going on, and then she would even take the fall for her team.

### Selling dreams and trusting your gut

Jeanette believes there isn't just one thing that makes a good leader. Different businesses require different types of leaders and leadership styles at different points in their journeys. The leader Momentum needed five years ago when they brought her and Hillie back is not the same kind of leader they will need in the future.

'When I walked in five years ago and I shared my dream with the team and what I thought we could achieve, some looked at me and told me I was mad. A year later we had achieved more than those original targets,' Jeanette says proudly.

'It wasn't because we were chasing a target; it's because everyone on the team bought into our dream of what we could achieve together. Every person knew exactly what their role was in getting us to achieve that goal. Every person should feel that they own a piece of that success. Focus on doing the right things and the profits will follow.'

In none of the companies where Jeanette has worked has there ever been a woman more senior than her, so she has never worked for a female boss. She feels a sense of responsibility to help turn the situation around and therefore tries to ensure that whenever she leaves a company, women will get the opportunities they deserve in senior management.

'By now, you have probably realised that I'm not a token appointment and similarly I won't offer anyone a position if I don't think they have the potential. As a woman, I feel the need to work a little bit harder and be more prepared because 30 years ago a woman was not expected to be in the boardroom. And it is good to have the right attitude. I once walked into a meeting and was asked to pour the tea, which I gladly did – and then I introduced myself. There was no point in embarrassing the gentleman because once he realised his mistake he was embarrassed anyway.

'I often advise young black professionals that if they walk into an organisation and find that it is totally white, they should not think that "people like me don't make it in this organisation". They should think, "what an opportunity this is". That was my attitude when I started at Momentum. I thought to myself that they are going to need strong women in leadership positions soon and when that time comes, I'm going to be so ready. That is how I got my first break; I was appointed manager at the age of 24. Today, I still feel the responsibility to spearhead change because our executive committee has only two female members.'

Jeanette has no children of her own, but she is a very involved aunt with 11 nephews and nieces. They have started working and are very serious about maintaining a work–life balance. 'I say that's okay, but you should know that if you want to be great at something, you're going to have to roll up your sleeves and work for it. In South Africa today, for every job that we advertise, we get thousands of applications and all the applicants have a degree. When we create a shortlist, we compare marks because at that stage your university marks are all we have to compare performance.

'I will not appoint someone who scraped through with 50%. That is simply not good enough. You must show me that you care enough about yourself and your career that you did your best to stand out from the crowd. I need to know that when your boss has a crisis and needs you at 21:00, you're the person who can be counted on. You need to stand up and stand for something and be somebody.'

Jeanette once met one of the business moguls implicated in a recent case of high-profile corporate fraud in South Africa and he made her skin crawl. Everyone else was filled with admiration, but her gut told her this was someone you shouldn't do business with. Because intuition like that flows from a collection of experiences but is intangible, it's hard to take into account for business decision-making. 'It cannot be entered on a spreadsheet,' she says.

'With my gut a million things come together, consciously and subconsciously. For instance, every three years I take a different female student and mentor her. She works with me, and I give her exposure. Michelle often asks me how I know to pick the right candidate, but I always just know.'

### *Approaching infinity*

Jeanette spends a lot of time on aeroplanes and on her own and therefore reads a lot. She loves fiction by writers such as Jo Nesbo and Patricia Cornwell, where you can never guess who the murderer is. She also indulges in business and leadership books, with her top recommendation in this category being Simon Sinek's *The Infinite Game*.

She says the book made an impression because it showed her that everything is infinite. She gives the example of striving to become a CEO, which is a finite goal. 'So, now you're the CEO but then you suddenly want to be the best CEO ever and there is no such thing. Even if you have these finite goals, everything is still infinite. If you pin all of who you are and your happiness on a finite goal, you'll never reach it because by the time you get there, the goal posts would have shifted again.

'I've read the book about five times because it encourages me to focus on leaving a legacy. What will I be remembered for? Instead of aiming for CEO, it should be about the state in which I leave the organisation and how people will feel about me and so on. If you pin everything on finite goals, you'll never feel fulfilled. But you can approach infinity through growth, being a decent person and being a leader.'

A book that has really helped Jeanette when it comes to how she thinks about leadership is *The 5 Love Languages* by Gary Chapman. Sure, it's not a business book (it is a relationship guide for couples), she says, but the description of five different ways in which people express love (gifts, acts of service, quality time, physical touch or words of affirmation) has taught her that people communicate in different ways and that they should be managed differently. It is up to her to figure out what personality type they are and how to bring out the best in them.

'The last book I would recommend is Sheryl Sandberg's *Lean In: Women, Work, and the Will to Lead.* It taught me that women can also be at fault [for not getting into leadership positions]. It's not always because men don't give us opportunities, but because we don't lean in, we don't trust our voices and we don't stand up.'

If given the opportunity to lead Momentum, Jeanette says she will give it her everything. After active service, she hopes to continue contributing as a board member. She finds the quality of board members in corporate South Africa to be quite poor. Many are 'consultants and academics with wonderful things to say but who have never led an organisation'. Consequently, their contribution is quite theoretic but holds little practical value. With her business experience, Jeanette believes she could hold the management of organisations to a high standard of delivery should she be appointed as a non-executive director in her later years.

People close to Jeanette know that she stocks plenty of wine and is a soignée fashion queen who always steps out elegantly dressed. You would think her ideal down time is spent in a bustling metropolis like Milan or New York. Instead, she lets her hair down on weekends and heads to their farm on the West Coast where she roams the plains barefoot with canine company. She doesn't have any fancy breeds; they are all rescue dogs.

At the heart of it, she is a farm girl, and nothing grounds her better than the simple things in life. Her best ideas and inspiration for business come from listening to the sounds of the ocean, chirping birds and lowing cattle while breathing in the earthy country air.

EY

# AJEN SITA

*A CEO who focuses on company culture*

'It is easy for competitors to copy what you've developed.
But if your differentiation is embedded in your structure,
it takes them a long time to replicate it.'

Ajen Sita shakes my hand firmly when we meet for our interview.
We're at the coffee shop in the foyer of the EY (formerly Ernst & Young)
building in Sandton, Johannesburg.

'What can I get you?' he offers warmly. I order a cappuccino, he a
latte. As we sit down to chat, it is immediately clear that Ajen knows
that people and the culture they create in a company are fundamental to an organisation's success – two of the three things Trey Taylor
focuses on in his book on corporate leadership, *A CEO Only Does Three
Things*. (The third thing, which Ajen has down to a tee being the CEO
of an accounting firm, is looking at numbers.)

It's as if Ajen and Trey Taylor speak from one mouth. 'Culture is
something that is written into the DNA of a company. It's part of your
very fabric; it's not something that changes at its core,' he says as we
sip our coffees.

Taylor writes that a CEO cannot create a culture through decree;
they should affect and shape it over time. He believes it is a company's
best competitive advantage as it impacts on every aspect of the business.
As the leader of the organisation, the CEO is responsible for aligning
the company's culture with the shared values of its employees.

With a strong company culture, you attract talented people who
perform exceptionally on behalf of the business, which, in turn drives

EY's **Ajen Sita**
*(Photo: Courtesy of EY)*

growth in your numbers. Without a strong company culture, the best people leave and the ones who stay are unlikely to act in the best interests of the business.

According to Ajen the fundamentals of what makes EY have remained intact over the years. In fact, he describes himself as 'a product of the EY culture'. It is a quality that has helped the organisation in the absence of rules, policies or systems that force people to act in a particular way. What culture does is that it provides a guide, a reference and a sense of direction for people as to what is acceptable in the company environment, he says.

'Culture helps people make decisions about right and wrong. It goes beyond being a negative policing thing,' Ajen says. 'At EY, we've tried to use culture to foster a sense of belonging so that people can identify with the organisation and what it stands for and still be unique as an individual.'

One way in which they have done this is their 'I am EY' campaign, which has been very visible on social media. The campaign features different employees telling their unique stories and the impact they are making in line with EY's payoff line of building a better working environment. The key message is that at EY, employees are more than just their work: they are also individual 'dreamers, adventurers, football fans, musicians, performers and more'.

## Agility and strategy

During our interview I was reminded of something Peter Drucker, the legendary Austrian-American management consultant, once said: 'Culture eats strategy for breakfast.' While a CEO should prioritise getting the company culture right, it does not mean strategy should be left behind.

Ajen knows this all too well, which is why a big chunk of his time goes into strategising. 'Many people think the choices they're going to make and the priorities they will set are what define strategy,' he says. 'To me, the essence of strategy is actually its context. It is about understanding the external market, changing trends, patterns, dynamics, expectations of our clients and society as a whole. Everything that we then bring to the table has to match that after we've understood our resources and capabilities.'

To Ajen setting a strategy should not be a one-off event but rather a dynamic process during which one constantly keeps an eye on the market, being agile enough to respond to changes in a practical way. He strives to come up with ideas that will allow EY to be more competitive in meeting the needs of their clients not only in the immediate outlook but also long into the future.

'Over time most of a company's products will be copied by others, so you have to ask whether you can build a level of agility into your system. For us, this involves creating a learning culture in the organisation and teaching our people to ask better questions. Our business sells the cumulative knowledge of our people, so we want our employees to always invest in themselves, also beyond what they learnt at a university.'

To this end, EY has programmes of ongoing learning and dedicated learning time that is set aside for each employee. Employees are encouraged to explore how they can harness technology better, how they can be more efficient and how they can better meet clients' expectations. EY serves a wide range of clients, from entrepreneurs and non-profit organisations to large private-sector companies and government entities. Because the heart of their strategy is meeting client expectations, it's crucial to ask their clients the right questions.

Ajen points out that to be employed at EY, you need at least one degree. This has certain implications for his leadership style. 'It means that as CEO, I'm dealing with some incredibly smart people who, from an early stage, have inculcated this culture of learning as a core part of who they are. They question everything and often seek to understand why things work in the way they do.'

It must have been a combination of strong leadership and this culture of critical thinking that kept EY out of the Zondo Commission's reports – the only one of the big four auditing firms in South Africa that was not mentioned. During this judicial commission of inquiry into allegations of state capture, corruption and fraud in the public sector, chaired by judge Raymond Zondo, the South African auditing profession was in the news for all the wrong reasons.

Ajen is clearly very proud of EY's good reputation. 'We faced a difficult operating environment during the state capture era. We saw firms taking on work, while we were turning away certain clients. This had an adverse impact on our business growth, but four years later, it's turned out we made the right calls and our reputation has remained intact, if not stronger than before. This has given us credibility with prospective recruits and clients.'

However, he is also keenly aware that reputational damage to any of the audit firms in the market, big or small, local or international, hurts the profession as a whole. 'Such news hurts the brand of auditing and accountancy; even prospective staff will be cautious about entering a profession that has been involved in controversy. We are working collectively to rebuild trust in our profession because we are serving public interest. We are the custodians of the capital market system and, by extension, the country as a whole.'

## Starting a one-stop service

Another way in which EY has succeeded in formulating and executing strategy is their integration on the continent. In the run-up to the 2010 FIFA Soccer World Cup tournament in South Africa, multinational companies were looking to set up shop in Africa. Similarly, South African companies were beginning to expand northwards. What businesses realised was that individual country economies were often small and that they needed to think about destinations as regions rather than singular nations.

'So there was a big structural change in the way we operated as advisors to business. Over an 18-month period, commencing in 2010, we integrated all of our businesses across sub-Saharan Africa into a single leadership team,' Ajen explains. 'As a result, we had one strategy, one structure and one operating model so that our clients, irrespective of where on the continent they went, would experience the same level of service. Similarly, the career experience was the same in the sense that learning, working methodology and promotion criteria were exactly the same. This made skills transportable across the continent.'

According to Ajen clients appreciated that EY offered a true one-stop service.

EY also realised that many African countries did not have good data to inform investment strategies for companies trying to figure out where to spend their money. So they commissioned the Africa Attractiveness Survey. 'This positioned our firm as the go-to destination for investment advice on the continent. It's quite easy for competitors to copy someone else's product. But if your differentiation is embedded in your structure, it takes them a long time to replicate it. By integrating all our African firms into one entity we got a headstart and it took others in our market over five years to have a similar model.'

### Being part of change

This first-to-market advantage resulted in EY writing a lot of business on the continent. Of course, with success comes responsibility, and the management team had to consider how they were going to effect change and stay true to their purpose of building a better working environment. They were aware of the many challenges Africa faces – poverty, unemployment, illiteracy – but realised they had to select one cause to champion.

'What stood out consistently for us was the poor representation of women in business everywhere on the continent. In light of our level of influence when dealing with governments and large corporates, we realised that we actually could have an impact. We challenged all the programmes we were involved with to support female empowerment.

'For example, our Next Gen programme, which is in its tenth year, is aimed at high-school children from poor schools. The girls in these schools have great potential but no access to opportunities. We've been giving them targeted support and today we have many graduates from that programme in different professions.'

Of course, gender diversity remains an issue in many businesses and as with many other things, the right leadership can have a great role in driving change. Another EY initiative, called Entrepreneurial Winning Women, assists female-led start-ups with training and access to high-value networks.

### Ajen, the person

I had met Ajen briefly before at EY's World Entrepreneur of the Year Awards before the pandemic put a stop to physical meetings. As we drink our coffees during our interview, my earlier impression of him being a 'people person' is confirmed.

Later, Nikki Benfield, EY's brand, marketing and communications leader says the same thing. 'Ajen is a happy person who loves to interact with staff. I always joke with him and say I don't want to work with any other CEO after him. So, when he retires, I have to retire,' she laughs.

'He really has a very good handle on the business. At times his inquisitiveness can be frustrating; sometimes our team thinks we've thought through a campaign and when we present it to him, he comes up with brilliant questions that we haven't even thought of. He has a knack for bringing the right people to the table and for such a busy guy, he is very approachable!'

Ajen has received many accolades. In May 2019, the University of Johannesburg named him a Professor of Practice and three years later the South African Institute of Chartered Accountants awarded him their Chairman's Difference Makers Award for leadership in business.

But he's not stopped learning. He completed a three-year course in philosophy through the Vedanta Academy's online programme (his daughter currently studies at the Academy in India) and likes to think of himself as a lay philosopher. 'It kept me busy during lockdown. I also bought a pizza oven and learnt how to make pizza – my son thinks there is no other food group in this world! And my wife taught me to paint.'

With this pizza-making philosopher professor, EY has a man of many talents at its helm.

# MIKE BROWN

*When hard work and luck combine*

'If you get the sense that you are growing, and working alongside
like-minded people with similar values and culture,
you have probably found the right place.'

My interview with Nedbank's CEO Mike Brown made me think of Paulo Coelho's classic *The Alchemist*. I got the sense that the man sitting across the table is someone who understands the value of finding one's purpose through the journey of life – just like the boy Santiago in Coelho's novel did. And like the wise people along Santiago's path who encouraged him to pursue his dream, so too Mike wants the upcoming generation to discover the power of persevering along their course.

Mike has been with Nedbank for 27 years, with almost 20 of those spent in the C-suite – starting with his appointment as CFO in 2004 and then taking up the top executive seat six years later. His career is proof that following your professional legacy could simply be a matter of finding the right company and the right job.

'I'm an advocate for staying in an organisation if it is in an industry that excites you and keeps you intellectually challenged,' he says. 'If you get the sense that you are growing, and working alongside like-minded people with similar values and culture, you have probably found the right place. If that is not the case, I'd advise you to leave and keep looking for the right fit. Your career is best served by working at an organisation long enough to show that you can deliver on ideas from conceptualisation to conclusion.'

NEDBANK's **Mike Brown**
*(Photo: Courtesy of Nedbank)*

In his role, Mike sees many CVs. He gets nervous about hiring people who have changed employers multiple times and prefers candidates who have a track record of seeing something through from start to finish to end.

He says in big organisations with many different divisions employees generally have a wide range of opportunities to find their fit, which can be valuable in developing one's career. At Nedbank, for example, they have business in private, retail and investment banking and asset management that is spread across Africa, London and the Channel Islands.

'With so many careers within the group, you'll find your niche if you stay in our organisation long enough. Personally, I've never been bored working in financial services.'

Mike says it's this sense of fulfilment, hard work and a dash of good luck that helped him get to where he is today. 'There's no substitute for hard work to get to the top. But being in the right place at the right time does help.'

What Mike calls good luck is likely, in Coelho's words, 'the universe conspiring to help him' along his journey to the top – in many small ways.

In the late 1990s, he dabbled with the idea of leaving Nedbank to pursue an opportunity at a start-up investment bank. But the new business ended up being less successful than what the predictions were, and his decision to stay at his first home turned out to have been for the best.

Then, a few years into the new millennium, the management team at Nedbank changed dramatically. At that time, Mike was three levels down the pecking order, but the shake-up in the structure seemed to have worked in his favour and allowed him to rise through the top management ranks fairly fast.

Towards 2010, not long after the world started to emerge from the global financial crisis, the CEO position opened up. By that time Mike had worked in both the front and back offices of the bank and, having been the CFO tasked with decisions around capital, liquidity, interest rates and risk management, he had skills that were top of mind for shareholders and board members during the crisis.

### On IQ and EQ

Mike advises professionals to invest as much as they can in their education because he sees it as the ticket to long-term success – something he's experience first-hand. Winning the award for the best final-year accounting student at the University of Natal (today the University of KwaZulu-Natal) in the early 1980s set him up for several future opportunities. He worked hard from day one, making sure he was the best prepared person in the room at every meeting, getting into the office earlier than others and leaving later than most of them.

However, he is also acutely aware of rising to the top requiring more than just brains and hard work. 'Life is about balance. People pursuing analytical professions like engineering, mathematics and accounting often have the IQ [intelligence quotient] but lack the EQ [emotional quotient]. To work in a team and lead people, you need that to have an emotional connection with them. Enjoy[ing] success only in business but not having a rich social, spiritual and family life will not be fulfilling.'

Mike is the chief executive of a bank with 27 000 employees and nearly 8 million customers. He sees it as a tremendous responsibility to lead an organisation that, as the custodian of savings, has an important role in society and offers a key mechanism for capital transition into the economy.

In 2020, he was voted Sunday Times Business Leader of the Year in South Africa by his peers. 'This is an award for which you are nominated and then the CEOs of the top 100 companies vote on their preferred name,' Mike explains. 'Maybe timing had something to do with my getting many votes. It was at the start of the pandemic and I was chairman of the Banking Association [of South Africa]. Our industry played an important role in ensuring that the financial system continued to operate.

'As COVID hit, several commentators predicted that we would have a health crisis, an economic crisis and a financial crisis similar to the [2008] global financial crisis. We did have a health crisis and an economic crisis, yes, but not the financial crisis. In fact, our financial system has remained remarkably strong and resilient. Banks were able to provide unparalleled support to their customers in those difficult times, which, in turn, had a massive impact in terms of supporting the economy.'

Looking back over the course of his career, Mike says having worked in both operations and finance has been valuable. When he first started out at the bank, he worked in the client-facing environment of treasury and structured finance, then moved to private equity and eventually ended up running the bank's commercial industrial property business. When he was appointed as CFO, he moved to what some consider the 'back office'.

'Some CFOs do not transition to the CEO role because they're quite happy to remain in a finance role and have no aspirations to lead the organisation as a whole. But those who are curious about life experiences outside their area of specialisation can move into the CEO role and make a success of it.'

### A focused strategy

During Mike's time as CEO, Nedbank has continued strengthening its brand. The group has quite deliberately moved away from a multibrand strategy to a more focused one, consolidating their resources behind a single message. As a result, they have seen big gains in their brand valuation and market share.

'I think what's front of mind for most people when they think about Nedbank is that it's a bank that stands for sustainability. Anything to do with green – that's us. It's not just our corporate colour; it is in our DNA.

'We have also been working really hard over the last six years to shift our digital positioning dramatically, and the data tells us that the digital journey Nedbank has been on is currently perceived by many as market leading.'

These gains are thanks to an effective strategy, which Mike believes must be contextualised within a company's current reality with regard to operations, resources and the external environment in which it operates. It is equally important that the strategy can easily be explained and executed.

'I see a lot of strategies that are wonderful on paper but too complicated to get over the line,' he says. 'In my view, a strategy must be focused on achieving a competitive advantage. This concept is rather transient, so your strategy must be able to absorb shifts and respond accordingly.

'Over the past 20 years, I have also learnt that timing is crucial. In the early 2000s, part of our strategy was to be at the forefront of the convergence of banking and technology. However, this has played out meaningfully only in the last five years. We had the right strategy, but we were probably about 15 years too early when it comes to how financial services have evolved. It is only now that things like apps and consumer adoption of technology are accelerated. Back then companies presented impressive ideas for solutions, which they were in fact not able to provide. They were hoping to work alongside us to develop the technology.'

While their technological strategy has paid off, Mike also knows that in business things don't always go as planned. For example, Nedbank's investment into the rest of Africa has been difficult and slow. In Southern Africa, their strategy has been to own and control their own banks in Namibia, Eswatini, Mozambique, Lesotho and Zimbabwe. They have a minority stake in Ecobank, a market leader across West and Central Africa. But the last five years have been difficult in these regions because of the drop in oil prices that put a lot of pressure on almost all West African businesses given the reliance on oil in those economies.

'With the current rise in the oil price we expect the environment to be more buoyant, but in the past few years it's certainly not been so rosy. In hindsight we probably could have been more astute in terms of the timing of our investment in Ecobank, given the high congruence between oil prices and its underlying performance. It's difficult to get your timing right, because you never quite know whether you're at the top of oil prices. So when oil prices fell, it became clear that the underlying businesses were not quite as strong as we initially thought.'

## Leadership and management

Mike views the key to leadership as understanding company culture and values. It is about listening and being empathetic towards employees because in complicated roles nobody has all the answers. At the same time, it is important to get employees to buy into the company's vision and show them a promise of a better future. He believes this is the way to galvanise and inspire people to want to be part of the journey the company's leadership has set out on.

Management, though, is more of an operational concept, he says, as it focuses on things such as excellence in service delivery. While management is important, it is strong leadership that really takes an organisation to greater heights, because it allows for people to accept change within a disciplined management structure.

Mike believes that of the many hats a CEO has to wear, three are key to success. The first one is to ensure that the business is performing well for clients, staff and shareholders. This entails offering clients value and coming up with new products, ensuring that valuable staff are retained and new talent is attracted, and delivering good returns to shareholders.

'The second hat is that of transformation, which is about the visionary role of leadership. It comes down to identifying the next big mountain everyone will climb together and outlining why we would want to climb it in the first place,' Mike explains.

Then there's the third hat, which is about culture and values. 'The CEO is the custodian of an organisation's culture and values, which, in many businesses, embody the "magic" of what makes the business work. If leadership gets the culture and values right, they end up with an extraordinarily successful business. The opposite is also true: in most, if not all, of the corporate failures we see, a weak culture lies at the heart of the problem.'

Nedbank's strong company culture is one of their key competitive advantages, Mike believes. 'Our culture is driven by people-centred behaviour: respect, integrity and accountability. It's not based on short-term thinking, but rather seeks to build something that will be good for the long term.

'This aligns with my own values, which I think explains why I have stayed at Nedbank for so long. Many people will choose to stay with an organisation for long if they believe in its values and have colleagues who exemplify them.'

Future CEOs who want to embark on following their personal legend, should remember that corporate success and career longevity are only possible if you balance it with a happy personal life, Mike advises. He enjoys regularly playing 18 holes on the golf course and loves to visit the Kruger National Park with his family or spend a weekend on the KwaZulu-Natal north coast, where he grew up, whenever he can.

As a father of three, he always makes time for his family and over the years he's learnt that 'most work matters that seem very urgent are not necessarily so'.

# FAITH KHANYILE

## *The benefit of balance*

'Good leaders are bold leaders.
They need to be courageous when defining and designing a strategy
yet realistic about setting achievable goals.'

Although Faith Khanyile left her home in KwaBiyela outside Empangeni in KwaZulu-Natal at a young age to go study in America, it's the life lessons she learnt while growing up in this small village that laid the foundation for a successful career. When her father left formal employment at Spoornet, he and Faith's entrepreneurial housewife mom set up a shop, and the children were expected to help run it.

'Our parents instilled a culture of hard work in us,' she says. 'We were always top of our respective classes. We rarely had time to just laze around – even on weekends we had to wake up early to help around the shop. Boys and girls were not treated differently in our home; we all cooked and did the dishes. This helped me realise from an early age that I am no less capable than men. This is something that has propelled my career.'

Faith's parents also taught their six children that it's their responsibility to help uplift the community. They set an example by being involved in building schools in the vicinity and sitting on their governance boards, because they realised how much power an education has to change lives – perhaps because they themselves were not able to complete high school.

After matriculating from Ohlange High School in KwaZulu-Natal in 1986, Faith got a year-long scholarship to the Emma Willard School,

WDB INVESTMENT HOLDINGS's **Faith Khanyile**
*(Photo: Courtesy of WDB)*

a prestigious private preparatory school in Troy, New York State. The scholarship was sponsored by privately owned schools that were against the apartheid system and wanted to help uplift children from disadvantaged schools.

Her good grades earned her another scholarship, this time from Wheaton College in Massachusetts, where she graduated three years later with a degree in economics. Another scholarship followed, this time from the United Nations, which afforded Faith an opportunity to complete her MBA with specialisation in finance at Bentley University two years later in 1994, the year of the first democratic elections in South Africa. The MBA was courtesy of a scholarship from the United Nations.

With an MBA in her pocket, Faith returned home in 1995, the year after the first democratic elections in South Africa, and joined Brait PLC in Johannesburg as an investment analyst. The company had just launched a private equity fund in South Africa and Faith was one of its first employees. Her responsibilities included doing research and due diligence assessments on target companies the fund could invest in.

It was at Brait that Faith's relationship with Women's Development Business (WDB) Trust, a public benefit organisation, began. WDB was established in 1991 by former first lady Zanele Mbeki and a small group of women who wanted to be active participants in the new democracy.

'Brait helped WDB Trust to set up WDB Investment Holdings,' Faith explains. 'WDB Trust relied on donor funding to fulfil its mission to uplift rural women. The purpose of the investment company was to help the company become self-sufficient. With my background in private equity, I was selected to help structure a commercial vehicle for the trust.'

After about six years at Brait, Faith wanted to get a deeper understanding of investment banking and joined Standard Bank as a relationship manager in its corporate banking division. She later moved to the structured finance division, where she eventually ended up as director. In April 2008, she was appointed head of corporate banking

responsible for over 600 people in the business unit, where her responsibilities included driving strategy and ensuring that the division
became more client centred.

Faith's role here involved not only dealing with multinational cor-
porations looking to invest in South Africa, but also servicing African
clients outside South Africa.

## Investing for good

After more than a decade at Standard Bank, during which she also became the first black woman to be co-opted to the executive committee
(Exco) of its corporate and investment banking arm, Faith was ready for
a new challenge.

She decided to apply for the position of CEO of WDB Investment
Holdings, having been impressed by the work the company was doing
to uplift women in rural areas, an issue that was close to her heart.

'I joined the organisation when it was ready for the next level of
growth. We had to develop a strategy aimed at doubling the net asset
value and so we had to seek opportunities that we could exploit, using
our positive track record built up over 15 years, to achieve that goal.'

Apart from wanting to increase the company's financial value, they
also wanted to have an impact beyond uplifting just rural women. For
instance, they were looking to influence the companies they invested
in to transform so that more women would participate in leadership. In
addition, they started thinking about setting up a youth development
programme and getting involved in education through offering study
bursaries to underprivileged young people.

'When I came back to WDB Investment Holdings, I realised we needed to strengthen the board and get more independent members with
commercial experience. I then worked with the executive team to
develop a strategy, that once approved by the board, could be broken
down into specific deliverables to help us achieve our financial and
social impact goals. One of these involved raising capital, because doubling net asset value would have been impossible without funding.

'We also had to recruit a suitable team that would help us deliver on the strategy and execute the plans that we had set out, so that we could report to the board on a quarterly basis. These reporting sessions helped us to monitor our progress and there were often suggestions for how to course-correct when things were not going as planned. Annual reviews kept our strategy dynamic so that we could adapt to changing market conditions.'

There were several curveballs during Faith's tenure at WDB Investment Holdings, including a volatile political environment during the Zuma presidency and the COVID-19 pandemic. The company managed to increase its net asset value by 80% instead of the doubling they had aimed for amidst the political instability and consequent uncertainty.

The situation also changed how they deployed capital, pushing them to diversify their investments away from only listed companies. They targeted growth sectors, such as fast-moving consumer goods, private healthcare, private education and fintech, and also expanded their portfolio into neighbouring countries with higher growth rates, for example by making investments in affordable housing in Botswana and Namibia.

Investing in unlisted companies enabled them to take meaningful stakes of more than 25% of the shares. This meant that they were in a position to have board seats and could influence transformation.

## Putting others first

Good leaders are bold leaders, says Faith. They are courageous when it comes to defining and designing a strategy, yet also realistic about whether the goals are achievable. The best leaders, in her view, are those who manage to find a balance between being brave and accepting reality.

'A good leader also acknowledges that leadership is all about the people,' she says. 'People must be at the centre of what you are doing. You should be interested in their development because without a team that is inspired, motivated and engaged, you're not going to be able to achieve your objectives.'

Faith spends much of her time coaching and exposing employees to challenging situations. 'If you do not stretch people, you will not influence their growth. You must delegate tasks and trust that people are capable of them.

'Leadership is also about remembering that it is not about you; it is about the stakeholders you serve – your clients, shareholders and communities. It is about putting their interests ahead of your own, which requires humility and a mindset of service. In addition, a leader must be willing to learn because no single person can claim to know everything.'

Looking back, Faith says the highlight of her career was being involved in founding and later running WDB Investment Holdings. During her tenure as CEO, the entire board was led by women and the company paid out tens of millions of rands as dividends to shareholders. She is also proud of the impact the company has had on women, young people and the unemployed.

'We had a programme to incubate unemployed graduates and we managed to induct them as full-time employees in the companies we invested in. Our success rate in this regard was over 90%. It's rewarding to think that a small team – we were only about 13 people – could be involved in bringing about impactful social change. The graduates we started bringing in around 2016 really needed mentorship because they came from families where nobody previously held a white-collar job.

'I'm also proud of the bursaries that have enabled underprivileged students to attend university. We partnered with the Oprah Winfrey Leadership Academy for Girls, where most of the children are from rural backgrounds. It is heart-warming to know that we were able to change the direction of their lives, which, in turn, also positively affected their families and communities.'

When I ask Faith about the lows of her career, she talks about seeing how the COVID-19 pandemic impacted a number of the companies WDB invested in. She fears that some of those in the education and service sectors may never recover.

'Another low was having to retrench people at Standard Bank,' she laments. 'Where people are let go because of poor performance you can at least rationalise it by saying they had an opportunity to do better but failed to do so. But with retrenchments, you take away bread from people's mouths through no fault of their own. It is incredibly difficult, because at some point you may even have interacted with their families and then you have to tell them that you are going to take away their source of livelihood.'

## Life after WDB Investment Holdings

In May 2022, the company announced that Faith had resigned to pursue personal interests and spend more time with her family. She continues to chair the WDB Growth Fund, a separate fund of which shareholders include WDB, Standard Bank, the Jobs Fund and Ascendis Health and which focuses on supporting small businesses.

She is also a non-executive director of Discovery, Bidvest and the Johannesburg Stock Exchange (JSE). These seats hold serious fiduciary responsibility, she says, and she takes time to read and understand every aspect of the board pack late into the night. The appointments she has accepted are for companies whose vision and mission align with her own and she is passionate about how she can contribute to overseeing their strategies.

To Faith, there is no set way to define success; it depends on what drives a person. 'For some it is financial success, for others it could be something else. For me success is defined by how I feel at the end of each day. I reflect on whether I achieved what I set out to do and whether it is aligned to my purpose. The sense that I am fulfilling my goals is what tells me whether I am successful or not.'

Part of success is also about having a positive impact with your actions. Reflecting on women in leadership, Faith observes that there have been some positive changes in the corporate landscape, but that much can still be done. Of the JSE-listed companies, women make up approximately 20% of the board members and 6% of CEOs.

'Considering women make up 51% of the population, it is quite sad that we are so underrepresented in corporate leadership, especially when research shows that entities with diverse leadership perform better. I have resigned from some boards because I realised the companies were not serious about transformation. They claim they are unable to find women who are capable of being directors, but my view is that they are not trying hard enough.'

Faith may have resigned from WDB Investment Holdings, but she will be a lifelong champion for women's rights, as her views on the gender pay gap show. Women, on average, earn less than men for doing the same work. To be part of driving societal change, WDB Investment Holdings has therefore partnered with the International Women's Forum and South Africa's Businesswomen's Association to advocate for legislation to address the problem and they are also running campaigns to counter the social structures that result in gender inequality. Away from work, Faith loves learning new things. She is back in the classroom learning Hebrew as part of her embrace of the Kabbalah discipline. She recently took up mountain biking and she also loves running. Given her driven and hardworking personality, it comes as no surprise to learn that she has completed the Comrades Marathon three times.

# JJ NGULUBE

*The courageous expert*

'Courage is what separates managers from leaders.'

I first approached John Junior 'JJ' Ngulube for an interview early in 2013 for an article in a magazine I had founded, called *The Expatriate*. He flatly refused.

Despite my explaining that the magazine aimed to capture the stories of professionals from other parts of Africa who lived in South Africa, he said, 'I am an African. I can't be an expatriate on my own continent.'

Months later, I returned to him with the news that the publication had been renamed *The African Professional*. He finally obliged.

At the time he was CEO of Munich Re and I visited him in his spacious office in Johannesburg. I learnt that if life had gone according to plan, JJ would have been a farmer somewhere in southern Zimbabwe. But fate had other ideas – and in 2009 he was included as one of the world's smartest executives in the book *1000 CEOs* by business journalist Andrew Davidson.

JJ entered the business world through agricultural studies, obtaining a Bachelor of Science degree in agriculture at the University of Zimbabwe and a masters in agronomy from Pennsylvania State University, where he graduated in 1986. Between the two degrees he served briefly in Zimbabwe's Ministry of Agriculture.

He joined Munich Re in Harare in 1987 at the age of 29 and stayed with the company for nearly 30 years, after which, in February 2016, he moved to Sanlam to head its corporate business. JJ is now retired but

MUNICH RE & SANLAM's **JJ Ngulube**
*(Photo: Mzu Nhlabati)*

sits on various boards; he is a non-executive director of both Continental Reinsurance and Santam Limited and the independent non-executive chairman of Marsh Africa.

In October 2016, JJ was reassigned to the international side of Sanlam, taking over as CEO of Sanlam Emerging Markets, where he covered their business in India, Malaysia and the rest of the African continent. He retired in January 2021 at the end of his five-year contract.

Speaking to JJ almost a decade after our first interview, I notice that he still has a relaxed demeanour, which I suppose has contributed to his success as a manager. He reveals that an extracurricular activity he got hooked on in university must take some of the credit for this. 'I took up karate and improved to the level of black belt. The art teaches you to be aware of your surroundings. In the business environment this helps you to be prepared even for unpleasant eventualities … You learn to fight through difficult circumstances and to be calm when others are losing their heads.'

The father of three has since traded in his black belt and bare feet for golf clubs and lush fairways, boasting a commendable handicap of 10. He disputes the notion that when golf is good, business is bad. 'It is all about good hand–eye coordination and staying calm when those inevitable errant shots occur,' he insists.

## Mergers and acquisitions

JJ left Munich Re because Sanlam presented such an exciting challenge – the Emerging Markets business was a much bigger entity than Munich Re in Africa. When he joined, Sanlam had a presence in 14 African countries but this had grown to 33 by the time he retired. The growth strategy entailed doing acquisitions and establishing greenfield start-ups. The most significant acquisition during JJ's tenure was securing a controlling stake in Saham Finances, a group that had insurance entities in 26 countries in Africa and the Middle East.

JJ explains that Sanlam's strategy was to decide which markets they wanted to enter and then do the research to find out whether they held any interesting targets. When there were none, they would start a greenfield, if practical.

In big companies, mergers and acquisitions are conventionally driven by corporate finance teams who do target assessments, valuations, due diligence and negotiations. Often it looks straightforward enough on paper and the management team would be sufficiently inspired to continue with the acquisition. 'But the post-merger integration is where the rubber really hits the road,' JJ asserts.

'It's where the fun and games actually begin, because you have to do real business and work with real people. It is also the point where good deals can die. Of course, there are instances when the due diligence failed to identify all the risks, but even when everything checked out, integration is what largely determines whether the venture is a success.'

When JJ was driving the Saham deal, he established two workstreams. The first worked on the deal itself, while the other was charged with detailing what would happen in the business once the merger was announced. Running two parallel streams was important, because only the senior executives of the target were aware of the impending transaction, whereas the rest of the staff would find out only on the day the takeover was announced.

The kind of questions that arise during an acquisition include what the new owners intend to do with the business, what the structure will look like and where staff will be allocated to. Clients also want to know what the change means for the services they receive and therefore it is prudent to outline your priorities as soon as the deal is concluded.

There are different approaches to acquisitions, JJ explains. Many private equity players consider targets that are broken, but which they believe they can make a success of if they fix one or two things. In other cases entities are targeted because they are successful and turning a profit, and an acquirer is looking to own that business without making too many changes. Although many commentators advise that the new owners should appoint their own executives to establish authority, JJ believes that if there are good people running the business, such a shake-up is unnecessary.

## Leadership takes courage

When I ask him about the highlight of his career, JJ doesn't hesitate: it was being appointed CEO of Munich Re Africa after he started off in the business as an underwriter. It was always an ambition to run the Africa business one day.

But there were disappointments too, like when the company's shareholders decided to close down Munich Mauritius in 2015. 'It baffled me that they decided to shut it down,' JJ says. 'It was a small entity, but consistently profitable. However, when converted to euros, the profits were small and therefore the European shareholder decided that it wasn't worth the trouble. That was a disappointing moment for me, having watched the entity grow from when we started it in 1998. But as they say: there's no room for sentiment in business.'

JJ believes the key ingredient to successful leadership is courage – business leaders must be able to make tough choices. 'I think the appropriate term is "call" rather than "decision", because the word decision suggests that you have all the necessary information. Often a leader is making a call based on judgement rather than complete information. That takes courage and self-belief.

'When you are a leader, you should let your teams handle the day-to-day activities, while you focus on making the big calls. That's where courage comes in, because change is often difficult. I always say: "Only a baby with a wet diaper enjoys change".'

Courage also means being able to decide on a route other than what your team thinks is right. Even though leaders should listen to the input of others and take it on board, they need not always agree with the majority, says JJ.

He also points out that in business certain calls must be made early on, because if you wait until you have all the required information, it might be too late and someone else could have beaten you to it. A leader is supposed to see the opportunities and take a business into the future. That's why the job also involves sharing your vision with your team and getting them excited about the possibilities.

'When we acquired Saham we spent $1 billion for a 54% stake and we had to convince the team and the board that it was worth spending that amount of money,' JJ recalls. 'It wasn't easy, because we had our critics. Analysts wrote long articles in which they said every South African insurer who had gone into the continent had failed and they insisted that Sanlam would be no different. If you don't have courage, you would read those damning narratives and decide to back down. Courage is what separates managers from leaders.'

In this regard, JJ often reflects on Nelson Mandela. Soon after the first democratic elections in 1994, the ANC hierarchy was pushing for the removal of sports emblems like the Springbok. After much debate, Mandela decreed that since the party chose him to lead, they should allow him to do his job and that the Springbok emblem would stay. Two years later, the Springboks won the Rugby World Cup at Ellis Park – a unifying moment that would not have been possible if Mandela had lacked the courage to push back.

### Strategy

Like many companies in the insurance industry, Saham Finances was negatively affected by the COVID-19 pandemic. Sanlam Emerging Markets (now known as Sanlam Pan Africa) also experienced challenges in places like Angola, Lebanon and Morocco. To JJ these were not unexpected during such a turbulent period, and in South Africa, for example, the short-term insurance industry was hit by an avalanche of contingent business interruption claims.

'I don't think you can say we made the wrong decision [to acquire Saham Finances] because of what happened afterwards. A decision is correct based on the information you have at the time. When we decided to acquire Saham, there was no way of predicting that a global pandemic was on the way. It was a good acquisition because Sanlam is now in an unassailable position on the continent.'

'I would rather have a mediocre strategy that is well executed than a brilliant strategy that doesn't get out of the starting blocks. Consultants can come up with all kinds of stunning presentations and CEOs also like to wow their boards with flowery language and grand plans. But then, once approved, the strategy is often not fully executed. I prefer a simple strategy that is ruthlessly executed.'

At Sanlam that meant acquiring companies and running them with local partners who have the necessary skills to drive those businesses. A core team based in Johannesburg, Cape Town and Casablanca supports the various countries. For example, if an entity has to change its software, the team flies in and supports the migration. This frees the people on the ground to focus on growing the business. It's a simple, executable strategy, says JJ.

Besides supervising mergers, the transition from reinsurance to insurance was an interesting one for JJ. A reinsurer is like a wholesaler, who doesn't deal with the actual customer. In contrast, at Sanlam, they had to deal directly with the insured party, like a retailer would deal with a shopper. It was a dramatic change because of the granularity, volume of data and the speed with which decisions must be made. At Munich Re, JJ was used to the team receiving quarterly accounts and then sending or receiving payment depending on the assessment of the business performance in that period. At Sanlam, though, thousands of claims are received every day and clients want them processed quickly.

### Become an expert

A few months before my interview with JJ, I met his son Ndabenhle, one of twin brothers, at a birthday party for JJ's granddaughter at his home in Bryanston. Ndabenhle is one of the founders of Pineapple, an insurance company that does things rather differently. For instance, one can take out insurance on single items, simply by taking a picture of it, loading it on their app and then receiving an instant quote.

During our interview, I ask JJ if he ever advises his son on strategy.

'No, I certainly don't. I don't think he would necessarily listen to me because their business model is so cutting edge and he thinks I'm old school! In fact, his owning part of Pineapple is something I have to declare to the companies I am involved in because Pineapple competes with them.

'It is wonderful to see him make his own way successfully in the industry I spent my career in. As they say, the [pine]apple does not fall too far from the tree!'

Pineapple Insurance certainly does things in a different way, also in terms of their advertising. They announced themselves to South Africa with billboards that say things like '9/10 people who work at Pineapple would recommend our insurance. WTF Jim?' and 'If you type "insurance" into Google, you'll find us on page 3'.

Whilst JJ cannot advise Ndabenhle, he is happy to share some words of wisdom with other young professionals. 'I think it's important that you specialise in something; become an expert in what you do so that you always bring something of high quality to the table. But you also need to gain new competencies, because if you focus only on becoming, say, a brilliant engineer, you will have fewer chances of being a CEO of the company. You need a wider breadth of expertise and competencies. Once you have mastered your speciality, look for other opportunities within the business.'

He then gives an example from his own life. 'I was a crop insurance underwriter. If I had focused my energies only on that, I might've been the world's top crop insurance guy today, but I would never have risen to CEO. You need to add to your toolbox.

'In my case I got involved with the strategy of the business and later I also spent time in human resources, which is the most difficult job. It is easy to settle a claim of R50 million and then go to bed at night. However, if you are responsible for firing someone, you take that pain home and it will bother you for a very long time. I have heard people call HR matters "soft issues". That's bullshit. It is a lot harder than the other stuff we do.'

At Munich Re, JJ got to manage a global IT project for the group. Despite not being an expert on IT matters, he was willing to learn. He says good leaders are those who are not afraid to show subordinates that they do not know everything and are willing to ask questions. His advice is to get out of your comfort zone and learn different things.

This approach also helped to prepare him to serve as CEO, because when HR raised issues, he knew where they were coming from; when underwriting was talking, he could speak their language; and when IT made proposals, he had a good idea of what they were saying.

JJ's view on being in the top spot speaks not only of a fully rounded leader but also of one with courage, because only the brave will push themselves into unfamiliar territory and constantly be open to learn.

BUSINESS LEADERSHIP SOUTH AFRICA's **Busisiwe Mavuso**
*(Photo: Rapula Ramasoga)*

# BUSISIWE MAVUSO

## *An agent for change*

'Making no decision is worse than making a bad decision.
Leaders shouldn't let the fear of making an incorrect decision
paralyse them from making a call.'

Academically strong since childhood, Busisiwe 'Busi' Mavuso passed her matric with flying colours at Lofentse Girls High School in Orlando East, Soweto when she was only sixteen. In the year of the first democratic elections in South Africa, she gained entry into the then Rand Afrikaans University (today University of Johannesburg) to study accounting, but after three days on campus, her mother sat her down to share some upsetting news …

She had tried her best to raise the fees for Busi's registration and her first term's studies, but she had failed. As a widow on a teacher's salary, she simply did not have enough money to pay for Busi's university fees, educate her three other siblings and keep the lights on at home.

So started Busi's 23-year journey to realise her dream of qualifying as a chartered accountant. In mid-1995, she secured an apprenticeship at Allied Bank and started studying accounting through the University of South Africa (UNISA) in 1996.

It was a steep learning curve. The first time she touched a computer was when she started working and she was terribly worried she would break it! To keep up with her colleagues, she had to take the first bus from Soweto to Randburg and the last one back. She even had to work weekends to ensure that she didn't fall behind. Her long work hours also had an impact on her studies, and it took her nine years to graduate.

Looking back today, Busi realises she lacked proper career guidance. 'All I knew was that I liked mathematics and accounting in high school. I didn't know that to become a chartered accountant, I should have registered for an articles contract at an audit firm. By the time I figured that out, it was too late for me to leave banking and take the salary cut. As the first born, I needed my salary to pay for my siblings' education and contribute to our family's living expenses.'

Without an auditing training contract and the practical experience in an audit environment, Busi failed her honours degree. Determined to keep improving and empowering herself, she registered for a postgraduate degree in management at the Gordon Institute of Business Science, which she obtained in 2011. That was followed with a master's in business leadership at UNISA in 2015.

'It took me 23 years since I started studying accounting to achieve my childhood dream of qualifying as a chartered accountant. This was thanks to the UK's Association of Chartered Certified Accountants who credited me for my work experience. It saddens me that the South African association is not considerate of individuals from disadvantaged backgrounds who could not afford to study full time. There isn't a concerted effort to level the playing field and therefore it takes black people much longer to get into the C-suite than it does their privileged counterparts.'

The reason Busi so badly wanted to qualify as a chartered accountant is her belief that it is important to be a technical specialist in a particular field. Few organisations go out to recruit a generalist for a position; they are often looking for someone with a particular set of skills who they can later transition into a management role. She believes being a specialist is what separates you from other candidates during recruitment.

Busi is currently pursuing a doctorate in business administration through Universidad Católica de Murcia (UCAM) in Spain. 'I am driven knowing that failure is not an option. Even when I fail an exam,

I cannot throw my hands in the air and give up because I do not have a plan B.

'We had to be tough as nails when I grew up. Things were not as they are today for many of the young people who have a mentality of entitlement. Like Malcolm Gladwell says in his book *Outliers*, "we did not succeed despite our humble origins but because of them". Growing up with struggles builds a strong character to handle academic challenges and other adversities.'

### Decision-making and the 40–70 rule

Busi was appointed chief financial officer of the Black Management Forum (BMF) in January 2011 and promoted to managing director five years later. The forum is a member-based organisation that seeks to address the lack of representation of black professionals at top management levels in South Africa. Despite a marked increase in black women entering the workplace, white men continue to dominate the executive landscape owing to what Busi calls 'an artificial glass ceiling'.

In 2017, she moved to another membership-based organisation, Business Leadership South Africa (BLSA). Busi was appointed chief operating officer and was part of Bonang Mohale's succession plan, whom she replaced as CEO in 2019. At BMF, Busi championed black professionals in big business, but by joining BLSA she crossed the floor to start advocating for big business to have a conducive environment to operate in.

Busi can be described as a business leadership expert. One of her favourite leadership principles is the 40–70 rule, an approach used by former US Secretary of State Colin Powell. According to this principle, you need between 40% and 70% of the required information to make a decision. 'If you make a decision with less than 40% of the information, you don't know enough to make a good call. But by the time you've gathered more than 70% of the information, you would have taken too long to determine a course of action and your decision will likely be overtaken by events,' she says.

Making no decision is worse than making a bad decision, Busi says. Leaders are chosen for their ability to make good decisions, but they shouldn't let the fear of making an incorrect decision paralyse them from making a call when needed. Strong leaders rely on their gut and on previous experience to direct the people in their organisations.

### *Getting business more involved in society*

Leadership comes with a lot of power, but that power serves no purpose if it is not used, Busi argues. 'Leaders should consider how they are going to use their positions for empowerment. In South Africa, more must be done to redress the effects of apartheid. Business is a social partner with a disproportionate number of resources, which they are not using to create equality. The consequence is social instability – we have too many people with nothing to lose. The riots we witnessed in KwaZulu-Natal in 2021, when people went on a rampage looting and burning shops, [are] evidence of that.'

Busi notes that there is currently a big shift towards fulfilling environmental, social and governance [ESG] priorities in the corporate space. However, while companies are addressing environmental and governance issues, not nearly enough is being done to take care of the social priorities, she warns. 'A thriving economy is shaped like a diamond: the wealthy should make up 10% at the top, the poor must be at the bottom 10%, and the rest of people – 80% – should be in the middle class. In South Africa, we have a pyramid: an overwhelming number of unemployed people who make up the base. This is unsustainable for business because it also limits the number of consumers.'

Busi feels that big business in South Africa is 'an island of prosperity in a sea of poverty'. She is passionate about seeing this situation reversed and has been very vocal about it in her role at BLSA. She does not shy away from criticising the government for its actions and inaction. Too many CEOs of business associations do not stick their necks out, believing that politics is beyond their purview. Busi disagrees.

'We cannot ignore the political economy because politics is synonymous with economics. Business must make sure we have a seat at the table, because political issues affect us. Many find politics to be a sensitive matter, but it isn't because every decision by government impacts us. Every entity has three main risks: those relating to the country; industry risks; and risks associated with the company itself. The biggest issue we have at the moment is country risk and business needs to step up to help reduce it.'

According to the World Economic Forum's 2022 Global Risks Report, the COVID-19 pandemic worsened societal risks because of an erosion of social cohesion, livelihood crises and a deterioration in mental health. The report also found that the erosion of social cohesion presents a short-term threat to long-term priorities in 31 countries, including South Africa. The Johannesburg Stock Exchange is approximately 65% owned by foreigners and when they read the World Economic Forum's report, see the riots on TV and get wind of South Africa's energy issues they start to think twice about investing in the country.

Part of Busi's job is preaching the gospel of reform to make the country a viable investment destination. To this end, she has internalised BLSA's purpose of 'making South Africa good for business and making business good for South Africa'. Flowing from that vision and mission, BLSA has developed a strategy that Busi sees as a long-term plan.

'It is a work plan towards a desired future state that allows you to determine how to play and where to play,' Busi says. 'All businesses have competitors that operate in the same space and the question is how well you differentiate yourself. In this regard, you need to be agile to adapt to the marketplace because entities that do not change quickly get left behind. COVID-19 is a good example: companies that could not adapt to e-commerce lost out.

'But while agility is important, alignment cannot be ignored. You must always keep your purpose as an organisation in mind and not let marketplace prompts make you deviate from your true north.'

### Overcoming impostor syndrome

Busi might as well be spelt 'Busy' given how much she has on her plate. Besides leading the pre-eminent business leadership organisation in South Africa and pursuing a doctorate, she also writes two columns a week, one for *Business Day* and another for News24. She is a single parent to a 15-year-old daughter and an 11-year-old son.

'I work 18-hour days and have had to find ways to find balance. I'm not shy to ask for help and outsource certain tasks that I don't have time for. I've accepted that I cannot be everywhere at the same time, so having a driver and a tutor for my kids has been helpful. I am thankful that they understand my situation and do not blackmail me to be at each and every one of their school activities. They get the background I grew up in and what I'm seeking to achieve.'

Surprisingly, Busi says she is an introvert. When invited to business engagements, she would prefer to just sit in the corner and not speak to anyone. She can be antisocial and loves her own company. If it wasn't for her job, she would not leave the house.

'I think our brains know how to make the distinction between when we can submit to our preferred habits and when we are required to show up. My job requires me to network and I think I do it quite well, because I've learnt this skill. But away from the office I prefer to just stay at home, relaxing and taking the occasional walk. I don't enjoy travelling; in fact, I find it difficult to be in an unfamiliar environment.'

Busi regrets that it took her quite a long time to get where she is. Fifteen years ago, she was not very comfortable in her own skin and it took her a while to overcome her self-doubt. She frequently suffered from impostor syndrome, which Gill Corkindale defines in the Harvard Business Review as a collection of feelings of inadequacy that persist despite evident success.

Busi struggled to accept that she deserved her seat at the table. 'As a leader you cannot be in charge of situations if you're still seeking validation and affirmation. Self-doubt can be limiting, because you fail to put your hand up when you are more than capable of being selected for the leadership treadmill.

'I've had to fight to maintain self-confidence. In the words of [American motivational speaker] Denis Waitley, "it's not what you are that is holding you back, it's what you think you are not". Focusing on your weaknesses and not your strengths is like being left-handed and choosing to write with your right.'

In many ways, Busi has been shaped by the hardships she has had to face in her life. It informs her style of corporate leadership and how she views the role of business in society. It has also made her a force to be reckoned with and a voice that never hesitates to speak up when things go wrong.

# NIGEL ATHERTON

*The pursuit of re-invention*

'Ask your team for advice. It is crucial to surround yourself with
excellent people who, within their field, are more knowledgeable than you.'

As CEO of hospitality and entertainment company Peermont Hotels, Casinos and Resorts, Nigel Atherton is in the business of escapism and pleasure. But when it comes to running a company, you'll struggle to find someone more level-headed, realistic and hard-working than him. Peermont operates 12 properties across South Africa and Botswana, as well as the online sports and entertainment betting site PalaceBet.

'Gaming is a 24/7 high-energy industry, which I enjoy. But it's not for everyone. You must be willing to be on standby on weekends and having to work at night means that you can't do certain things during the day, like sharing a glass of wine with loved ones. Christmas, for example, is just another day for us and as CEO, I have to pop in and check on my people on that day.'

In many ways, Nigel is a self-made man. He is the son of a British fitter and turner who moved to South Africa when Nigel was seven years old. His family lived in Secunda, where his father worked in the machine shop at Sasol. After Nigel matriculated, he got a five-year training contract at KPMG in Secunda and by the age of 20, he was already managing the local audits of Sasol, gold mines and other feeder businesses in the area.

It was a good start in terms of professional experience to be a manager at such a young age, but it also meant that Nigel missed out on

PEERMONT's **Nigel Atherton**
*(Photo: Courtesy of Peermont)*

the typically carefree university years and never had much of a social life, because his focus was on completing his distance-learning accounting degree, starting a career and then starting a family. Even though he found commercial law tricky, Nigel passed all his examinations at the first attempt and qualified as a chartered accountant in 1997.

Nigel explains that in Secunda, most qualified people move into the accounting department of Sasol or to one of the mines. But life had something else in store for him. 'There is a lot of coincidence in life,' he says. 'Just as I was looking for a change, the government began granting licences to casinos and Graceland opened in Secunda. I joined them in January 1999 as an accountant and was later moved to the head office of Global Resorts [today Peermont].'

However, in the long run Nigel didn't enjoy the head office experience as he was involved in historic reporting rather than any of the major decisions being taken in the business. In 2005, he joined Zenprop Property Holdings but only stayed for a year as he found the property sector quite slow compared to the hustle and bustle of casino life.

In 2006, Emperors Palace invited him to join their finance department, where he worked as CFO for five years before becoming the complex's general manager in 2011. 'It is the best casino in the country and worthy of being called the "Vegas of Africa" ... There is rarely a boring day in the gaming industry and if I'm having a difficult time at the office, I can always walk to the floor and chat to customers, which gives me perspective and helps clear my head.'

In 2015, Nigel was appointed joint acting CEO of Peermont alongside Thabo Mokoena. But this presented several challenges, including that it created two centres of power and two different visions, and as a result the team did not know whose instructions to follow. The matter was resolved within a year and Nigel was appointed as CEO.

In his ascension to the role, Nigel consistently had to re-invent himself in new positions. As CFO, his role involved managing risk and he often had to be the handbrake to any potentially damaging business decisions. As general manager he was front of house, engaging with customers and focusig on revenues.

'At times you have to deal with very upset customers because the business model of a casino is quite unique,' he says. 'A customer at a supermarket goes in and walks out with tangible products, whereas in the casino business we are selling an experience and escapism. The customer may walk out with nothing, which can lead to buyer's remorse. It takes time to understand what the customer is feeling, and you must be very empathetic in your engagements with them.

'As CEO in the head office you may not always be aware of what is happening on the casino floor on a daily basis. You have to trust the people who work for you. The further up you go, the more reliant you become on the system, which is why it is so important to have good people that you can trust.'

## *Highs and lows*

In 2017, Nigel was involved in restructuring Peermont's equity and refinancing its debt, a first in his career. There were also plans to list the business, so it was a very busy period. From a revenue perspective, 2019 was the best annual financial period in the company's history, although Nigel points out that for any growing company each new year should potentially be your best. However, he remains proud of their performance in 2019, because today's hospitality and entertainment customers have a wide variety of options, and it requires hard work to remain their preferred choice.

The group has also signed a number of hotel management contracts, but has had mixed success. In a contract like this, the owner of a hotel appoints a management company to run the property on their behalf. In 2014 the group entered into a hotel management agreement in Malawi, and even though 'it was a good learning curve for Peermont', it walked away from the contract after five years.

'Hotel management might sound easy, but it has its challenges. Once you fix the problems, the owners think they can now manage the business themselves and then they cancel the contract after the initial period. If you don't fix the issues, then the hotel doesn't do well and so they fire you anyway. It is a lose-lose situation,' Nigel explains.

Since Peermont opened its casino doors in the 1990s, they've never had to close them or retrench any employees. Having to do both these things in 2020 was one of the worst experiences of Nigel's career.

What was expected to be a two-week interruption turned out to be an exceptionally challenging two years. From having up to 20 000 people on the property each day and about 900 staff, Emperors Palace went to having only a few maintenance and security personnel on site. 'Walking through Emperors Palace was like a scene from one of those movies where a shopping centre is abandoned and there are just a couple of kids on skateboards criss-crossing the yard. It was surreal.'

At the same time, management couldn't give up, but had to keep talking to customers to keep them interested in future entertainment options. Months later, when Peermont was allowed to reopen their venues, they had to keep modifying their operations as the government's COVID-19 directives kept changing. Nigel found the regulations 'challenging and often illogical'. He also had to support employees who dealt with heartbreaking personal tragedies. He recalls asking a staff member once how they were doing, and the person responding by sharing that they had just lost their seventh family member to the pandemic.

### Knowing when to take a step back and when to take the lead

The South African hospitality industry faces many challenges, which calls for strong leadership and a clear vision. Peermont, for example, is looking at ways to achieve energy independence and securing steady water supply through solar energy infrastructure, battery solutions and boreholes.

Nigel believes a good strategy is something a leader believes in and is aligned to their sense of achievement and personal values. Your broader team should also buy into and be willing to deliver on the strategy. 'You need the resources to support the strategy because simplicity, belief and empowerment of resources are what makes it all work,' he says. 'One of the lessons I have learnt along the way is the importance of asking your team for advice. It is crucial to surround yourself with excellent people who, within their field, are more knowledgeable than you.'

He also says a CEO should be willing to make difficult decisions and to implement them quickly. Already in his role as general manager, Nigel didn't hesitate to take the lead when the moment called for it. When conflict broke out between two factions at a conference that was held at Emperors Palace a few years ago, he didn't leave it to the security team to defuse the situation but took the microphone despite his introverted personality. It was nerve-wracking, but to his great relief he managed to restore calm.

While Nigel has often worked long and strange hours, he believes in the importance of a work–life balance. 'CEOs must give employees space, both at work and after hours. During the COVID pandemic it became easy to call employees late at night or when they were off duty, but you should rather let things that are not urgent wait and give teams time to recharge. Work should be work and home should be home. That way, when a colleague calls at an odd hour, you'll know it is really important.'

This happened one night over a year ago when Nigel got a distressed call from the general manager at Mmabatho Palms in Mahikeng. He just said, 'Boss, it's bad!' A fire had broken out at the complex and soon after Nigel received photos of the damage that had already been done. The hotel had burnt to the ground and initially panic ensued because six of the hotel guests could not be accounted for.

Nigel jumped in his car and drove all the way from Johannesburg to the North West capital. On his way there, he was informed that the province's premier had convened a press conference and he was expected to have an answer ready. It was an immensely stressful experience, but thankfully by the time he got to Mahikeng, the missing guests had been found.

'Profits can plummet and material things can be lost, but the worst thing that could ever happen to a leader is to lose a life on your watch. I am also glad that we were able to redeploy all our staff and no employee lost their job.'

### Dropping the 'Big Boss' front

For Nigel, an important quality of good business leadership is being able to reprogramme and reinvent yourself. For example, when you are in a junior role your work is likely to be quite technical and hands on, which will require you to learn certain skills.

When you get to the corner office, though, the focus is on the big picture and about guiding people to ensure they are headed in the right direction. This is when culture and values become especially important – it is the CEO's job to ensure that everyone is on the same page, he says.

CEOs should not be placed on a pedestal or put on a 'Big Boss' front, Nigel warns. Everyone has their shortcomings, and CEOs should not be afraid to show their vulnerability.

It is also a real problem when junior team members do not have the confidence or freedom to engage on issues. He says it is important for an executive leader to be present and approachable; your job is to inspire employees to work towards a common purpose and to ensure that they feel positive about their contribution.

Nigel highlights another aspect of being a CEO: it can get lonely at the top. When something goes wrong in a business, a CFO can say it was the general manager's fault, who, in turn, can put the blame on the CEO. The buck always stops with the CEO, which means you are limited in who you can share your problems with. You can easily feel quite isolated. To counter this, Nigel advises top executives to make contact with peers who they can talk to when facing tough decisions.

### Striving for balance

Nigel tries to follow his own advice of achieving a work–life balance. It is important for him to spend time with his family. His eldest son has been diagnosed with bipolar disorder, a condition Nigel says can be very difficult to understand as a parent. You tend to wonder if it is because you were a bad parent.

However, once you get qualified people to help you and start following a process to understand the condition and to support your child, it gets easier. His son has learnt to live with the condition and makes his parents proud. The experience has taught Nigel humility and not to judge others until he understands their circumstances.

'My daughter is the complete opposite,' he continues. 'Where my son is good with his hands, my daughter is excellent at academics. She probably gets her love for reading from me, because I spend a lot of time indulging in news, current affairs and technology articles. When I do read for pleasure, it is always fantasy.'

When I ask him whether he has any book recommendations, he suggests reading *The 5 Love Languages* by Gary Chapman. 'It's a great relationship book that really helped me to understand my wife better,' he explains.

'I advise parents to spend time with their kids because they grow up and move away in the blink of an eye. Work hard and go the extra mile at the office, but ensure that you make time to relax with your family. Your definition of success will likely change as you go through different life stages: first building a career, then building a family and finally retirement.'

'Retirement?' I ask.

'Yes, eventually, but I am not there yet!'

GENERAL ELECTRIC's **Nyimpini Mabunda**
*(Photo: George Oosthuizen)*

# NYIMPINI MABUNDA

*A corporate warrior*

> 'In a task with many people responsible for it,
> everyone is hoping that someone else will make it happen.
> Things get done when someone takes charge.'

Nyimpini Mabunda grew up in a village called Rolle near Bushbuck-ridge in eastern Mpumalanga. It had no running water or electricity. His primary school studies mostly took place under trees with make-shift chalkboards.

In 1976, the year Nyimpini was born, political tensions such as the June 16 Soweto uprising were raging in South Africa. Nyimpini's parents decided to name their child 'warrior' in Tsonga – a name that is a constant reminder of the call to action to bring about change.

'I became a real fighter,' Nyimpini writes. 'I knew nothing would come easy in life, especially if you were among the most disadvantaged. Even among black people there were degrees of being disadvantaged. For example, township blacks living in Soweto and other former Transvaal townships, were – as a rule – better off than most because they were more than likely working and literate.'

I first met Nyimpini Mabunda at the 2022 Kingsmead Book Fair in Johannesburg. We were the only two panellists in a session called 'Strategies for success', which was hosted by Hwalani Mabaso of Standard Bank. The session focused on our two books; my debut publication *Masters of Money: Strategies for Success* from the CFOs of South Africa's Biggest Companies and Nyimpini's *Take Charge: Life Lessons on the Road to CEO.*

I was in awe of the man. He spoke with such flawless articulation that I frequently had to remind myself that I too was a panellist with views to share and not one of the audience members!

A few days later I attended one of the many book launches he had around the country. This one was a fancy event at BMW's offices in Braamfontein attended by over a hundred young, eager participants.

With a day job as the CEO of General Electric, along with other roles, such as chairing the US–South Africa Business Council, it was difficult to find time in Nyimpini's diary for an interview for this book. But he made it happen a month later – testimony to how organised he is. We pick up from our conversation from that first discussion as if it was yesterday.

### A book for the underdog

Nyimpini explains that he wrote *Take Charge* because he believes that there are many other people from an ordinary background like his who could rise to the C-suite. He figured if he shared his life story, it would show people that even if you attended a public school you can still become a CEO, and he also wanted to debunk the idea that you have to speak English with a certain accent to get to the top.

'People always told me how special and talented I am and how well I seem to be doing,' he says. 'I keep hearing these things and yet, growing up, I did not think I was exceptional at all. Where I come from, there are many people like me; I wasn't even the best student academically or one of the student leaders. I wrote the book to encourage others to come out of their shells and have the confidence to believe that they have something to offer.'

Most CEOs are former CFOs who have studied accounting and so many people think they cannot lead organisations if they had not gone that route. Yet having a Bachelor of Social Sciences instead of an accounting qualification did not stop him.

'My book is aimed at the underdog. To use a football analogy, it is for the likes of Lionel Messi, who was told he is too small to play football, too weak to take on defenders and too tiny to jump and head the ball as a striker. He defied the odds when he was given the chance and he became one of the best footballers of all times. There are many South Africans with the potential to become the Messis of the corporate world if only they believe in themselves.'

The title of his book was inspired by one of the company values at Procter & Gamble, where Nyimpini started his career in finance, and speaks to taking ownership. When there is a task involving many people, it can easily end up not getting done – everyone hopes someone else will make it happen. Things only get done when someone takes charge.

Nyimpini says he has great admiration for Procter & Gamble's policy to promote from within; they appoint graduates and grow them internally, instead of hiring senior people from outside. This means that historically the CEO is someone who has been with the company for many years and who understands their markets. Its policy means that Proctor & Gamble is very focused on career growth, but you still have to take charge of your own destiny, Nyimpini points out.

'My central thesis in my book is that career growth is an active process, and you have to be aggressive and intentional about it,' he explains. 'If you are passive and leave it to HR [human resources] or your line manager, you will end up on the sideline, wondering why things are not happening for you.'

### Doing things the right way

After publishing his book, Nyimpini had a number of speaking engagements, including at business schools to talk to MBA students. But he also spoke to undergraduates and youths who were struggling to find jobs. 'I feel strongly about being active in this space because there are a number of things I can help address, including skills mismatch,' he states.

'The world is changing rapidly and there are many people who have qualifications that are unsuited for the job market. We have other issues around inclusion and diversity that need to be addressed. We need to talk about these things and discuss how we can take charge in the context of all these changes.'

The South African economy is hardly growing and globally inflation is rising. As a result, many people struggle to find employment. According to Nyimpini they need to get the tools to take charge and start their own businesses. In this regard, his engagements extend to entrepreneurship expos and workshops.

'We also lack suitable career guidance in our schools. Our youth need to hear from experienced people like myself to help them think about where their talents lie. But my engagements are not about me speaking to people; they are interactive sessions where I am also learning. They really do help me to stay relevant and informed.'

Nyimpini challenges people at work, in his social environment and even at home to always look for new approaches or solutions when faced with a challenge. His drive to help people achieve their potential is one of the reasons for having formally embarked on a journey as an executive coach. He has benefited greatly from being coached and realised its transformational power.

In his foreword to *Take Charge*, renowned businessman Dr Reuel Khoza describes Nyimpini's journey as an 'odyssey characterised by momentous defining phases, bursting with lessons in adventure, entrepreneurship, management and business leadership'.

He admires Nyimpini preference to assemble 'a personal board of directors', which means that he surrounds himself 'with sapient corporate elders' who are bold enough to provide him with critical feedback and do not hesitate to point out his vulnerabilities. 'Occasional vituperative comment from seniors who care about your development will not necessarily harm. Look for areas where you may be vulnerable and heed germane admonition,' Khoza writes.

Nyimpini approached Khoza for the foreword because he wanted a moral authority and symbol of ethical leadership to feature prominently in the work. 'Unfortunately, a lot of people think that to take charge of your career and accelerate on the road to success, you need to do wrong things,' he says.

'Just look at the reports of the Zondo Commission [of Inquiry into Allegations of State Capture] in which many respected companies and professionals are being cited for misbehaviour. In addition, we've had several corporate failures. But a few people, like Reuel [Khoza], have worked at the highest level with government institutions and the private sector and there has not been even a single scandal around them.'

Nyimpini believes that including Khoza in the book sends the message to readers that one can be successful by doing the right thing. Furthermore, he provides an intergenerational perspective since he is already in his seventies and has years of experience and wisdom. 'I also like that he is a business leader in his own right and not a person who relies on his blackness. Reuel has always exuded competence, even before black economic empowerment policies were implemented.

'My view is that we should not rely on affirmative action for our success. If the laws favour you as a woman or a previously disadvantaged person, that should only be the cherry on top and not the substance of what you're capable of.'

As a business professional who has worked in many parts of Africa, Nyimpini has had to navigate various immoral business practices that often involve brown envelopes. There have been times when officials demanded bribes to release goods at ports or to authorise work permits.

'While unethical business practices are a reality on the continent, we should also be mindful of issues such as transfer pricing where we have big multinationals expatriating profits from Africa to Europe and the USA,' he warns. 'They are robbing their host countries of the opportunity to collect more money and drive development. These things are facilitated by sophisticated schemes crafted by consulting companies without regard for the impact they have on Africans living in poverty. It is totally immoral.

'Similarly, I fail to understand how a multinational company can send five successive expatriate CEOs to run a company, each for a four-year term. That is 20 years of failing to develop local competency or simply a misplaced view that as Africans we lack the intellect to run these companies. It is high time our governments put their foot down and insist on local CEOs being appointed.'

## Positioning and timing

Nyimpini once asked a CEO how he had made it to the top, seeking advice for how he could follow suit. The executive told him that aside from financial acumen, you need five qualities to become a business leader: a strategic mind, intellect, emotional intelligence, great stakeholder management, and the ability to mobilise support. Still, having these qualities alone would not guarantee getting to the corner office, his mentor said, because the essential ingredient is luck.

Beyond luck, Nyimpini has found that positioning is a very important gateway to corporate success.

'Your networks are important, but so are the things you are able to offer. Why should a company hire you? It's almost like dating. It's about your value proposition as an individual, but also about being at the right place at the right time. For example, say you notice there is a craze about China, you could do something simple like taking an online course in Mandarin. It is about being proactive about the things that matter right now.'

On the point of China, Nyimpini believes its rise has somewhat slowed and that there are other, more topical business constructs professionals should embrace as catalysts for their careers. 'At the moment environmental, social and corporate governance and digitisation are crucial to every business strategy. If you are not learning about these things, then you risk being left behind. Positioning is about being strategic, learning about what counts and ensuring that the right people know that you know.'

Nyimpini also believes that timing is important; you constantly have to assess where you are in life in a broader sense. A professional with schoolgoing children is at a different stage to one who has children at university. This has implications for the types of roles you can pursue. For instance, a person who is young and single should look to take up an overseas role because employers abroad are looking for people without families who do not need the kind of remuneration that caters for school fees or regular flights home.

'And if you're a woman, you need to appreciate that now is your time. I get so many calls from companies looking for people to sit on their boards; international companies are looking for women and local companies are looking specifically for black women. I repeatedly emphasise to the women I coach that they need to put themselves out there for selection. Timing is about being aware of what is going on in your environment and aligning your career growth accordingly.'

In the chapter 'Leadership through imperfection' in *Take Charge*, Nyimpini shares his thoughts on the decisions he believes would have to be made in the post-pandemic era. 'While we must adapt and find new ways of operating and strategies for doing business sustainably, there are limits to what we know about the future. Executives and business leaders are currently encountering operating conditions for which we have not been trained. In a word, it is imperfection.'

He ends his book by writing about his family: his wife Dr Mosima Mabunda, head of wellness at Discovery Vitality, is a constant source of inspiration for him. 'She is competitive ... despite my ten-year head start, she has promised me her income would one day overtake mine.

'Simple, innocent conversations can bring great enlightenment,' he concludes. 'We cannot forget our humanity. At home I am not a CEO but a father, a husband. My family demands quality time and a deeper entrenchment in these bonds can give me the joy and hope I need to pursue my core purpose.'

CURRO's **Chris van der Merwe**
*(Photo: Courtesy of Curro)*

CURRO

# CHRIS VAN DER MERWE

*The modest maverick*

'People should respect you as a person rather than
because of your position. People can only respect you as a
person if you serve them with humility.'

Chris van der Merwe is a man who loves to tell his story – of how he
founded the first Curro school with 28 pupils and built it into a listed
company. And why not? It is an excellent story to tell. On the day we
are supposed to meet online, the internet connection fails courtesy of
loadshedding at his home in Mossel Bay. This does not deter him, and
he immediately heads out in search of the nearest hummock where he'll
have cell phone reception. We end up talking for an hour with him
standing there, the sound of the waves and chirping yellow-nosed
albatrosses in the background.

Chris's father died when he was only three years old, leaving him
and his sister behind with their mother. He recalls a wonderful childhood in Goodwood, Cape Town despite what he describes as their
abject poverty.

His mother really believed in him and inspired a lot of confidence
in him, encouraging him to make something great of himself. 'I was
determined to make enough money to buy her a car,' explains Chris.
'That was my only motivation back then.

'I had a thirst for knowledge and a good mind for money management. When other kids would be given 10 cents, they'd go buy toffees.
But I saved my pocket money until I had about R20 with which I could
get myself a rugby ball. Looking back, I showed an entrepreneurial

spirit, and I could also set myself goals and had the discipline to pursue them.'

Chris might not have been an A-student, but he had the grit to achieve his goals. After qualifying as a teacher, he pursued a master's degree, writing his dissertation on electronic learning modules. He graduated in 1992 and started working as a teacher at Fanie Theron Primary School in Cape Town.

Always yearning for more, he got permission from the Inspector of Education to set up a private company to write electronic learning modules as surrogates for textbooks. He ran the venture with 60 other teachers and even though the business was not profitable (their goal was merely to provide a service), it greatly improved his business skills, including managing cash flows.

Next Chris decided to pursue a doctorate in education at Stellenbosch University. For his thesis, he investigated what an educational institution would need to be able to compete with the best in the field, whether locally or abroad. After receiving his doctorate, Chris applied for a job at the Western Cape Department of Education.

'Unfortunately, I was not successful,' Chris says. 'I sat with my wife, Stephanie, and we decided that the only way I was going to live out my dreams was by starting our own school. So I resigned from my position as a deputy principal at a primary school and took my severance package of about R240 000. On 15 July 1998, we launched the first Curro school with only 28 children on church-leased premises in Durbanville.'

### The early Curro years

From the outset, they wanted to respect the uniqueness of each learner. Curro encourages students to learn according to their aptitude, attitude and talents.

Chris also involved his fellow teacher and mentor, Eduard Ungerer, who agreed to be his partner. 'The model C schools [government schools in the 1990s that catered mainly for whites] were quite good, but there were far too few of them by the late nineties. It cost the state about R80 million to set up a good school and the running costs, including teachers' salaries, were quite high. It would take the state over 100 years to bridge the gap between good schools and those that were below par by setting up new schools in developing areas. Our impetus was to create affordable, quality private-school education.'

Today Chris is grateful that he didn't get the job in government, otherwise the Curro dream would never have manifested. At the time, however, he was rather disappointed because he was a young educator with a doctorate and in his view 'on top of his game'. He was only 37 and looking to make a difference. But perhaps they thought he was too young, he reflects.

'I had a drive to create something for the nation; in fact, I can tell you without doubt that I never started Curro with the intention of making money. I wanted to serve the country by initiating affordable private education. Ultimately, I became CEO and was paid good money, which made me feel like I had been rewarded for my hard work.'

Having never studied business formally, Chris had to learn on the job when he set up Curro. In the first 10 years, he was responsible for financial planning and the business model, while his partners handled the academic department.

The good thing about the teaching business is that Chris had many good mentors along the way. He was also a captain in the South African Defence Force when he did his mandatory military service in the 1980s, which taught him several leadership lessons.

'My mother was a widow who relied on my father's small police force pension. That definitely thrust me into a position where I had to acquire leadership skills quite early,' Chris says. 'I think my studies also helped with the development of leadership principles and ethics.'

When he was still a teacher, Chris found his salary insufficient to cater for his growing family and so he began thinking of ways to supplement his income. He built a few houses, including his own, and when he got an attractive offer, he would sell the property for a profit.

In this way, he started to understand property development and this knowledge enabled the Curro founders to build more schools.

### Expanding education, expanding a company

The first four schools (in the order in which they were established) were Curro Durbanville, Curro Langebaan, Curro Silver Lakes and Curro Roodeplaat. For each new school, Chris had to tote a begging bowl to the banks for finance. The founders had to put up their personal assets as security for the hefty loans. Eventually, Chris realised this capital model was not going to help improve education in South Africa.

'We needed to scale the business to bring about meaningful change,' Chris asserts. That was when Curro started to engage with investors at PSG, including founder Jannie Mouton, from whom Chris says he learnt a lot. PSG decided to purchase 50% of Curro and also provided the company with a cohort of chartered accountants who shared many important business insights with the leadership team.

'Today Curro has 180 schools on 75 campuses. We simply did not have enough money to achieve this on our own, so when PSG came to see us, we proposed a 50-50 partnership that would help pay off our debt and build many more schools. I also supported listing the company on the Johannesburg Stock Exchange because being listed on the bourse would give us even more access to capital.'

Chris points out that being listed also helps to market your company because people then start to believe that you are a solid business. Today, at 60, Chris looks back proudly because it is a relatively young company that has achieved so much and has the potential to do even more.

Curro had a small teacher's college in KwaZulu-Natal called Embury Institute for Higher Education and a few years ago PSG, as a major shareholder, approached Chris to unbundle Embury from Curro and list it separately. During a particular strategy session, Chris presented a proposal to put 10 colleges together in one successful business and everyone agreed that it could work.

Today Stadio Multiversity has about 40 000 students. 'Because I got to the end of my career at Curro in 2017, I thought we would get someone else to run the business. But PSG asked me to lead Stadio for three years to establish the fundamentals of the company, including delivering on the prelisting statement's first promises. We believed we could replicate the affordable private education model at a tertiary level by creating a system that was predominantly online.'

Chris finally retired in March 2020. 'When I get on my knees to pray at night, I thank the Lord that I was chosen to lead this wonderful company, which has been able to widen access to education in the country.'

When Chris was still CEO, he loved to speak to the market regularly. But over time he has learnt to listen more and speak less, he says. There was also a time when people criticised the Curro model and insinuated that the company was simply out to make a lot of money. Chris regrets that at the time he didn't explain better that the money was used to improve facilities for their students.

'In any case, shareholders are entitled to dividends and therefore profit-making is not unethical. However, I regret not being more vocal about our position. Rather than keeping quiet, I should have amplified our intentions more in the media. Maybe growing up in a home without a father made me a bit of a softie. I should have explained to the world that you cannot provide quality in any sector without money.'

Chris doubts that school education will radically change in the aftermath of the COVID-19 pandemic. In fact, he believes the pandemic demonstrated that a campus that has the right systems in place can be extremely resilient during such a dramatic event. Parents realised that their children could carry on with school as normal for that time by having their lessons online.

The pandemic also helped educational institutions to streamline their systems to be more effective. For example, at Curro a master teacher in the group can now stream lessons online to multiple classrooms.

But at a tertiary level, campus-driven education might see an impact, he reckons. He foresees that universities will have to adopt a hybrid model, with more instruction taking place online rather than being limited to only on-campus learning. That means universities will be able to enrol many more students, which could have the added benefit of making tertiary education cheaper.

### On what makes a good leader

Chris believes you cannot be a good leader without having a clear vision, one that you believe in. He connects leadership to entrepreneurship, stating that a leader entrepreneur identifies a need and pursues it with passion. Passion eventually empowers you to get through the difficult times.

Also, to be a good leader you must be a good orator. 'I see many leaders who are such hard workers, but they struggle to communicate the positives in their companies in a clear and inspirational way,' Chris observes.

'A good leader is also a servant. People should respect you as a person rather than because of your position. People can only respect you as a person if you serve them with humility. I am a strong believer in servant leadership; I never rate the teachers in our organisation lower than myself. We are at the same level.

'People say it gets lonely at the top, but I never experienced that. Whenever I encountered something difficult, such as business forecasting, I would seek help. I would always start the day with the then financial director, Bernardt van der Linde [today chief operating officer], because I knew I had many shortcomings when it came to finance and accounting. The moment you let your staff experience the ways in which you need them, your job as a leader is half done. You should bring together different skills from different people and it's also important to stand firm with your team when trouble comes.'

On the question of strategy, Chris says country context is key. One should consider the state of the nation to establish the challenges and opportunities. Chris, who is extremely positive about South Africa, believes one should be driven by the need to help people rather than to make money.

'If you aim to address the challenges to help to make the country a better place, then your ladder is leaning against the right wall,' he proclaims. 'Start small and allow your business to go through an evolutionary process. Do not think for one moment that you are going to reach business success in a year or two. Draw up your strategy with the principles of quality and honesty in mind because that's what will get you far.'

For Chris success is about having a passion and being suitably qualified to pursue that passion. He says he would never have been able to create Curro if he didn't have experience in the education sector.

'Success is also about setting goals and achieving them. Every year, my family gathers around a table at our holiday home in Mossel Bay and then we write down our goals for the following year in a black book. This unites the family behind one vision and gives each of us specific responsibilities if we want to achieve our family goals.'

I ask him about lessons he's learnt from life. 'Money isn't everything; it's merely an enabler,' he answers. He also believes it is important to have a faith from which you can draw your values. Giving back to society is important, as is having fun. Furthermore, be purposeful about having 'me time' by planning holidays and other exciting activities outside the workplace.

Chris's crowning achievement of his career was the day Curro Holdings was listed on the stock exchange. 'I stood there humbled that a Grade 5 teacher can go from teaching 28 kids at a rented church to the CEO of a listed company. Another high was Curro being ranked third in the Sunday Times Top 100 Companies competition in 2016. The competition looked at the companies that had delivered the highest return to shareholders for five consecutive years. We beat some of the country's biggest brands!'

While these memories clearly bring Chris immense joy as we talk, his voice becomes progressively more tremulous in the outdoor chill. I finally release him back to his waiting family with the promise to chat again soon.

# SANDILE ZUNGU

*The African industrialist*

'We need to move from a developmental state to a developmental society
where entrepreneurs have to address underperformance
in areas traditionally served by government.'

Two things are instantly revealed by Sandile Zungu's Twitter profile, @mfanawasemlazi. Firstly, it shows how proud 'the boy from Umlazi' is of where he was born in 1967. The township, southwest of Durban, is the fourth largest in South Africa and the only one with its own car registration plate, NUZ.

Secondly, it gives an indication of his appreciation for his Zulu heritage. In Sandile's profile photo he is dressed in an indigo blue suit, perfectly matched with an off-white shirt. The formal corporate attire reflects his status as one of the country's top businessmen. The look in his eyes is piercing, determined. A leopard-skin *umghele*, a traditional headband, rounds off the picture.

Although the picture only shows his upper body, it clearly suggests that his left knee is bent and his right foot is raised. He has the slightly crouched stance of a warrior readying himself to pounce. In his left hand is a large oval-shaped shield and he holds a chiselled staff with a whip made of the tail of a Nguni cow in his right.

Sandile's father used to work for a refinery and his mother was a nurse at a local clinic in Umlazi. He was but 10 years old when he was first introduced to the basic principles of entrepreneurship. His father brought home from the refinery drums filled with rejected petroleum jelly. His mother, in turn could get used medicine bottles at the clinic

ZICO's **Sandile Zungu**
*(Photo: Courtesy of ZICO)*

and together they started a business that sold bottled jelly to township customers for use as an elementary ointment.

Sandile's weekends were spent painstakingly cleaning the bottles and filling them up with the jelly. Umlazi was quite safe at the time and Sandile and his siblings would go door to door selling the bottles. He quickly learnt a few important business skills, including how to negotiate competitive prices, how to know when you can extend credit to someone and also how to collect debt.

Sandile's parents were religious and also placed a big premium on education. They sacrificed much to ensure their children went to school. 'We simply could not disappoint them,' Sandile says. 'I was one of the top students in my school and in 1984 I got a scholarship from Shell to do a post-matric [year] at Hilton College. Then they paid for my mechanical engineering studies at the University of Cape Town [UCT]. I graduated in 1988 and the following year I joined Richards Bay Minerals as an engineer.'

### Starting his own company

However, after six years, Sandile realised engineering was not his calling; it was not something that excited or enthused him. In 1995 he went back to UCT to do a one-year MBA. His intention at the time was to move from engineering to marketing, but when he got to UCT, he discovered his real passion was for finance.

'Studying finance subjects piqued my curiosity. In 1996 I joined a merchant bank that was a joint venture between American investment bank Donaldson, Lufkin & Jenrette and New Africa Investments, subsequently renamed African Merchant Bank [AMB].'

AMB were the corporate financial advisors to Super Group Limited when the company was seeking a listing on the Johannesburg Stock Exchange and Sandile was part of the team involved in that onerous process. He also had a pivotal advisory role in what was the biggest black economic empowerment deal at the time, the acquisition of Johnnic Communications by the National Employment Consortium.

It was a watershed transaction involving many big names, such as Cyril Ramaphosa, Patrice Motsepe, Wiseman Nkulu and Phuthuma Nhleko, all of whom Sandile got to meet.

However, during that time he realised that he wanted more than being an advisor; he wanted to become a principal with his own investment company. In 1997, he took up a position as the head of the South African Railways and Harbours Union (SARHU) Investment Company. The arrangement included a 5% interest in the company, which gave him a solid base as they made investments in several sectors. His success in growing the company's investment portfolio and generating handsome returns over a three-year period made him believe he had the ability to run his own shop.

In July 2000, on his way to Boston, USA to join the global leadership programme at Harvard, Sandile met Dikgang Moseneke, then CEO of New Africa Investments Limited. Moseneke had heard about Sandile's experience in mergers and acquisitions and invited him to help with the merger between Sanlam and Momentum (the investment company was supposed to be the controlling shareholder of the merged group). Sandile grabbed the opportunity, but unfortunately the merger did not go ahead following the death of Marinus Daling, Sanlam chair and the person driving their negotiations.

At this point, Sandile felt it was time for him to finally launch Zungu Investment Company (ZICO), which he accomplished in 2002.

'My first deal at ZICO was to buy SARHU Investments' stake in Isikhonyane Cleaning Services, which was a joint venture between SARHU and the Fidelity Services Group,' Sandile recalls. 'I paid R100 000 for it. It was a small investment for SARHU, which they saw as a nuisance. But it made sense for me to buy it to establish a relationship with Fidelity – I knew Fidelity would one day need an empowerment partner and I would be well placed to fill that role.'

Within three months, Isikhonyane managed to declare a dividend of R250 000 to ZICO, meaning Sandile more than doubled the cash he had paid in a financial quarter. ZICO grew rapidly and soon had a turnover of over R45 million a year as it secured cleaning contracts with the owners of big buildings such as the Reserve Bank and the Carlton Centre in Johannesburg. So when Fidelity Supercare services decided it was time to do an empowerment deal, ZICO was the obvious choice. Sandile's vision had paid off.

ZICO paid R4.6 million for a 25% stake in the company in 2005 and this turned out to be a very profitable investment. In addition to receiving annual dividends, they disposed of their shareholding for R125 million when Compass Group acquired the investment in 2012.

Sandile went on to execute even bigger deals, including the purchase of Anglo American's stake in Seriti Coal in 2017. Two years later, Seriti acquired the coal assets of Australian mining company South32. 'The resulting company, Seriti Holdings, is now worth over R20 billion. It is a dividend-paying company, which makes it a wonderful addition to our investments,' Sandile says with a smile beaming across his face.

While ZICO has seen great success, it has also faced tough times. In 2017 the company bought into Elgin Engineering, a business rescue on which ZICO spent over R100 million trying to turn it around. They sadly failed. Elgin's main client was the Engen refinery, but it was closed down after a massive fire in December 2020. Its other clients were in the sugar industry, which had been hit hard by punitive taxes and sugar being dumped in the South African market by foreign players.

Sandile views Elgin as an isolated case, though. 'Overall, we've done quite well. Apart from Seriti, there have been many more deals that have resulted in exits at between R150 and R200 million after we had invested less than half that amount and got dividends prior to disposal, such as Viamax Logistics, Taquanta Asset Managers, Goldrush Gaming and AutoZone.'

### On black economic empowerment

I ask Sandile whether he thinks it is fair that only a few big players seem to be benefiting from empowerment deals. He responds by saying he believes true entrepreneurs like him would have been successful regardless of the transformation policy.

'BEE [black economic empowerment] is an enabler, but it is not the only thing that propelled me to success,' he says. 'It was also not conceptualised to empower millions of people. There are other schemes that are meant to benefit a broad base of people, such as those by MTN, Multi-Choice, Sasol and Vodacom. Ordinary people have made a lot of money out of these schemes by investing hundreds of thousands and exiting with a couple of million. These schemes have empowered many people.'

When the policy was transformed into broad-based black economic empowerment, Sandile and other industrialists were critical of it out of concern that it would create the expectation that a vast group of people would suddenly become rich. It had to be clarified that 'broad-based' means the criteria for black economic empowerment would be expanded to include more than black ownership and would also take into consideration corporate social investment, enterprise development, management control and affirmative procurement.

'There is no capitalist economy where every single person is an entrepreneur or businessperson. Some people are more than happy to earn a salary and to go home after a long day and do other things without worrying about work. We have created a misplaced notion that everyone would become rich and, when it doesn't happen, we resort to blaming the so-called usual suspects [the seemingly small and exclusive group of black billionaires].'

According to him, the people who should make empowerment happen 'are those who got the gains by virtue of their skin colour through a corrupt and illegitimate system called apartheid'.

Sandile believes the share schemes that have been initiated by big companies and the successes of individual black businesspeople shows that black economic empowerment has been successful. 'My view is that BEE has worked, maybe not as well as it should have, but to think of it as a failure is ridiculous. Apartheid is the failure, because it created the morass that we find ourselves in. Yes, we can improve on BEE's efficacy and its instruments; we can tweak it to drive certain behaviours and certain outcomes, but it is definitely not a failed policy.'

Should it have a sunset clause? I ask.

Sandile says no. 'BEE is about ensuring that the economy reflects the demographics of the country. The sunset is not about time; the sunset is about outcomes. For as long as black people are in the margins of the economy, this thorn of BEE must remain ever present and prick the conscience of everyone. In my view we have not achieved the necessary outcomes yet. In fact, in the last couple of years we have taken our foot off the pedal, and we should be looking at ways to speed up the process.'

### Stepping in to help the country grow

Sandile believes South Africans must be dynamic in creating economic growth in the country and should not solely depend on the government to do so. We live in a world filled with new opportunities, he says, and the revolution in digital communications is in its infancy. 'We are part of many global networks experiencing digital disruption, which has already changed the way we live and will continue to upend old industries and create new ones.'

In his view, new business models and careers are going to emerge. Professionals and entrepreneurs should align their thinking accordingly. 'My advice to businesspeople is to consider a new logic. Our growth path has to be outward looking and based on exports. Given that we cannot create more internal demand, we have to grow by servicing the world and competing in it.'

He points out that key parts of the economic infrastructure, such as power, communications and transport, cannot be serviced by the state alone. 'We need to move from a developmental state to a developmental society, where entrepreneurs have to address underperformance in areas traditionally served by government.'

On a more personal note, he values the role of family in the lives of finance professionals and entrepreneurs. 'Business is not easy … you can be a tough person dishing out instructions at the office and making big decisions, but after hours, you have to have someone who will be a sounding board for you and who you can trust to be frank with you. Generally, it's your life partner who will point out things like having to tone down your words when you are being interviewed. The input of your family is invaluable.'

Sandile knows the power of personal and business networks. 'I did my MBA in 1995 and while I've probably forgotten most of the content of the course, what remains are the relationships with people I was in those trenches with. The programme I did at Harvard again introduced me to people from across the globe. Wherever I go in the world, I have friends who are only a Facebook message away from meeting with me.'

Coming back to his Zulu heritage, Sandile put his money where his heart is by investing in one of the great symbols of his community. In 2020, ZICO purchased AmaZulu Football Club from Dr Patrick Sokhela. The team is often a relegation candidate at the bottom of the premier league, and Sandile's desire is to transform it into a championship-winning side.

'The team is now doing extremely well; we hope they will be like a phoenix rising from the ashes. When King Zwelithini died in 2021, he must have had a smile on his face because he had seen the resurgence of his team. AmaZulu is a part of the psyche of the Zulu nation. So, as the Zulus mourn the king's passing, we try to provide tears of joy as a football team. We are playing our part in contributing to social cohesion in KwaZulu-Natal.'

Here is an African industrialist channelling his business acumen for community upliftment. South Africa could do with a lot more Sandile Zungus.

SAGE & PaySPACE's **Sandra Crous**
*(Photo: Madeleine Maré Photography)*

# SANDRA CROUS

## *The definition of an outlier*

'A lot of work goes into being successful.
What you put in is what you get out. It is not possible
to invest just a tiny bit and get out heaps.'

The people who make it to the top don't just work harder than anyone else, they work much, much harder. Researchers suggest 10 000 hours is the magic number for achieving mastery; the equivalent of three hours' practice a day over ten years.

In his book *Outliers*, Malcolm Gladwell cites a German study among violinists who all started to play around the age of five. The elite performers among them had totalled 10 000 hours of practice by the age of 20, those who were good about 8 000, and those who ended up as music teachers had done just over 4 000 hours. There were no 'naturals' who practised less but floated to the top, and no flops who did the 10 000 hours but failed to rise to the highest ranks.

Having worked in the payroll and human resources space for over 30 years, PaySpace managing director Sandra Crous has put in much more than 10 000 hours to distinguish herself as an outlier.

Is there such a thing as innate talent? Possibly, Gladwell concludes, but there can be no achievement without preparation, he qualifies. The closer psychologists look at the careers of the gifted, the smaller the role of innate talent seems to be and the bigger the role of preparation, he writes.

Sandra is a staunch supporter of Gladwell's philosophy. 'A lot of work goes into being successful,' she affirms. 'What you put in, is what you get out. It's not possible to just invest a tiny bit and get out heaps. Every evening, you should be able to look back at the work you did and feel proud that you gave your best. I advise young professionals not to wait for others to give them recognition or pay them a certain salary or confer a specific job title on them. Put yourself out there and, through hard work, earn what you seek.'

Sandra firmly believes that everything one does should have a purpose. 'If you're engaged in purposeful execution, success will undoubtedly follow. In whatever role you are placed, you can be an influencer; you don't need a job title. I've seen people having a massive influence in a company despite not being in the boardroom. I often bring lower-ranked employees into our management meetings because I want to see them grow and often they have ideas that make everything fall into place.'

### From telemarketer to managing director

Sandra's father was a primary school principal who worked hard to ensure his children got a good education. After matriculating, Sandra wanted to go into politics and enrolled for a degree at the University of Pretoria. But in the third year of her studies, one of her very close friends died in an accident. Grief stricken, Sandra quit campus to go look for a job.

She joined the South African Permanent Building Society briefly before moving to a start-up called VIP Payroll in 1989. Sandra started off as a telemarketer in the company that, at the time, had only seven employees. Over 27 years, she rose through the ranks at VIP Payroll, which later became Sage Africa.

Her rise to the top started after she was appointed as sales director and later took up the helm as vice president for Midmarket Africa and the Middle East. During this period, she oversaw significant revenue growth in the entire mid-market segment, augmenting the company's reputation and client base in Africa and the Middle East. Her becoming managing director at Sage counts as Sandra's biggest professional achievement. Looking back now, she says, the key to becoming irreplaceable is having focus in your career and making sure you become a specialist.

Since then she has also held positions in the education sector, most recently as CEO of both Damelin Online and the London College of International Business Studies.

In April 2019, Sandra was appointed managing director at PaySpace, which has thousands of customers in 40 countries and across more than 65 industries. The digitisation of payroll and human resources processes has been a big part of her career and the thought of innovating on a cloud-based, tech-first product through PaySpace really got her excited. In a world where timing is everything, there couldn't have been a better match between her own career goals and the aspirations of this rising player in the payroll industry.

'My focus at PaySpace has been to increase the business's market share throughout Africa. With more companies in Africa embracing digitisation and doing more cross-border business than ever, the legislative and compliance hurdles they face can be a serious risk. PaySpace has proven itself as a software supplier with successful statutory legislation across Africa, meaning that legislative compliance is assured, no matter where you are situated. This product really does cater to every market and that's what growing African economies need.'

### Creating a culture of trust

Sandra constantly thinks about how to attract new talent to the company and build a space where colleagues can reach their full potential. She also believes a leader has to set the example of what you expect of colleagues, which for her is high performance.

Leaders should not preach water and drink wine, she says. Indeed, those who have worked with her describe her as inspirational and passionate, as someone who is able to demand results simply because she herself is constantly concerned about doing the right thing.

'Whether you have an audience of a thousand or an audience of none, you should carry on with integrity. If you walk into the reception of your office and see the flowers on the counter are in disarray, do you fix them or do you walk by thinking it is not your job? The culture I strive to build is one where everybody understands individual progress is bred in collective success.'

At PaySpace employees work completely remotely. With that, Sandra expects every colleague to have their camera switched on for every meeting and she sets the example regardless of whether she has put her make-up on or not. She also requires colleagues to be engaged in the meeting and not to continue working. 'I don't mind if someone says, "Sandra, I will be right back, I've to take an urgent call." But that would be an exception.'

Working remotely means that everyone has to keep an up-to-date diary. They don't have to ask permission to visit the doctor, but it must be shown on their calendars. Furthermore, PaySpace has a rare human resources concept called 'limitless leave', which allows employees to go away for lengthy periods as long as the affected colleagues approve. Sandra explains that if an employee is passionate about their work and delivers consistently, others will have no problem with them taking leave and will also be respectful of their time away.

Since the company introduced the policy, people have started taking more leave than the 18 days they were previously offered. However, employees are much more engaged than before, says Sandra. According to their wellness survey in 2021, employees generally enjoy their job and love working for the company. The leave policy and remote working have helped build a culture of trust where colleagues believe no one reports to work to do nothing.

The company doesn't have annual performance appraisals but employees do have frequent discussions with management where they track their goals set in the previous meeting. As CEO, Sandra also asks employees how she can help them achieve their goals.

'We measure everything we do because we've got a culture of high performance and we see ourselves as a disruptor in the industry. We challenge ourselves every day and everyone is well aware of what we're building. When I do my monthly general meeting, I talk about what we have done and always try to link it to our vision, mission and values. For instance, if I thank someone for creating something. I'd highlight that it aligns to our value of innovation.'

## Conquering the market

PaySpace sales are growing over 30% annually, which is an amazing feat in difficult economic times. The reason the company is doing so well is that they're solving customers' problems by curing the inefficiencies in the software industry.

Sandra aims to grow three times faster than her competitors because she wants PaySpace to become a market leader. 'How we'll do that is very simple: we need excellent customer service, an extremely stable software product and an operationally efficient organisation.'

To scale the business, PaySpace measures customer service by keeping a close eye on its 'net promoter score' rating, which is a measure of how likely a customer is to recommend the business to a friend. And they're doing well: over 80% of their revenue is recurring, which has made the business very attractive for prospective investors. Sandra says if no one is looking to acquire your company, it's a sign that you've not built long-term value. These are some of the ideas she has gleaned from her two favourite business books, *The New Market Leaders* and *The Discipline of Market Leaders*, both by Fred Wiersema.

'When I started my career at VIP Payroll, the company founder made all of us read these two books,' Sandra reminisces. 'They offer valuable insights on entrepreneurial leadership, which has been proven in how VIP Payroll panned out. When I started at the company, we only had 30 customers. A few years later we had thousands. What the books teach you is that you must choose your customers and narrow your focus to dominate the market they're in.'

Market domination arises from ideals such as striving to be a product leader, as can be seen from the likes of Apple and Nike, companies that invest huge sums of money in world-class products. It can also be achieved by operational efficiency, meaning that delivery to the customer keeps them coming back even when the product is not that great. A good example is McDonald's: burgers are served within minutes of being ordered and taste the same whether you're in Bangkok or in Sandra's recently adopted hometown of George.

'A good business also has a common goal that everyone can chase regardless of their role. I even want our cleaner to understand that her role is part of building a world-class organisation.'

In the post-pandemic era, a lot of people are working remotely and 'dialling out', and it is getting increasingly difficult to keep people engaged, says Sandra. 'This is why you need the right people on the right bus: employ suitable staff, place them in the appropriate roles and inspire them with the company's mission.'

PaySpace is the kind of company for which the COVID-19 pandemic had some positive impact, because it is a single-instance, multi-tenanted software company. This means a company's payroll can be processed from anywhere. The pandemic accelerated the transition to cloud software and PaySpace has taken full advantage of it, introducing such rarities as leave applications via WhatsApp.

'In service of our customers, we have also abandoned the idea of them paying huge, fixed fees upfront. This has really helped in hard-hit industries. For instance, we have many clients in the entertainment space who had to retrench many of their employees during and after the pandemic. Our flexible billing allows them to pay only for what they use, meaning they save money during difficult times and can increase spending once business picks up.'

### Family first

Sandra's advice to female professionals is to avoid using their gender as an excuse not to achieve great heights. She is proof that women can do just as well as their male counterparts if they lead with their heart and have their head in the right place.

'And never let a corporate career get in the way of building a family if you aspire to have one,' she advises. 'There's never a good time to take maternity leave, so I would always advise a woman working for me to "simply do it now".'

Family should come first, Sandra says. 'You cannot outsource building a family as no one can teach your children family values better than you.'

Sandra might have been pivotal in taking a local South African business to global recognition but after decades of service, you won't find a statue of her on any corporate premises. That's why she preaches that no one should lie awake at night worrying about the company they work for. Her advice is to apologise for a mistake when it is made and move on. Take care of yourself because your employer would be better off with a balanced staffer than a workhorse.

Now in her early sixties, Sandra believes she is in the most productive phase of her life because she has gained so much experience. She is also a 'summa cum laude graduate of the University of Life', with lots to offer a business looking to be a dominant player in Africa. With plans to expand to other markets, such as Brazil and the UK, she cannot imagine retiring and doing nothing – business development is too exciting. While she may not run the comrades anymore, she is still very active and loves to go hiking in the mountains around George every weekend.

'Tell me one surprising thing about yourself,' I ask.

'I'm a very mischievous grandma,' Sandra laughs with a sparkle in her eyes. 'I break all the rules my children set for me. In the middle of the night, I wake up the grandkids and we creep into the kitchen for a midnight feast. They end up sleeping in my room and in the morning we share the same toothpaste (and it's not the low-fluoride nonsense my daughter insists they use). As kids, we used the same toothpaste as our parents and we turned out just fine!'

SOUTH AFRICAN AIRWAYS's **Thomas Kgokolo**
*(Photo: Thomas Kgokolo)*

# THOMAS KGOKOLO

## *The turnaround talisman*

'You should create an environment where employees feel that they are
allowed to make mistakes and that there is collaboration in steadying the ship.
Mistakes should be viewed as part of the learning process.'

In April 2021, Thomas Kgokolo was catapulted into the spotlight when he was appointed interim CEO of South African Airways (SAA). Within weeks, he went from lecturing students to having to explain to the nation what was happening at the airline and the reasoning behind their decision-making.

'Unlike with private airlines, everyone thinks they have the right to express an opinion on how the national carrier should be run. As the CEO of SAA you have to make yourself available to the media to explain to the country why you are making certain decisions. It calls for transparency and effective communication.'

But by then, Thomas had already learnt that being a business leader requires you to make difficult decisions and that at times you have to be bold.

Already as a young man, Thomas started reading books on money management, which made him dream of one day running his own business. He was the first of three children who were raised by his grandmother in Seshego, outside Polokwane, since his policeman father and shop owner mom both worked in Johannesburg.

When he had to choose between science- or finance-stream subjects in high school, he was torn, as he enjoyed science but was also intrigued by finance. However, his father advised him to go the commercial route, since he believed that financially it would be more rewarding.

Thomas emerged top of his class and was particularly good in accounting, a subject he soon developed a passion for. He was accepted at the University of Pretoria for a BCom Accounting degree and graduated in 2003. Thomas's family lacked the financial resources to let him pursue an honours degree but he got a learnership through the Banking Sector Education and Training Authority in 2004. He was placed at Standard Bank and made such an impression that he was offered a permanent position.

However, Thomas declined the position, opting instead to register for an article contract at the Auditor-General in Pretoria in 2005. He completed an honours degree in accounting through the University of South Africa (UNISA) and joined PwC in 2006 where he finalised his articles contract, qualifying as a chartered accountant (CA) in 2008.

Both in high school and at university Thomas had helped fellow students with their studies and really enjoyed doing so. This spurred him on to consider a career as a lecturer and he decided to take up the position of senior lecturer at UNISA shortly after qualifying as a CA.

In 2011, while still teaching part-time at UNISA, Thomas joined the audit committees of both the Mogale Local Municipality and the Mpumalanga Provincial Government. After a year as chief financial officer of the Competition Commission, he decided to pursue an MBA at the Gordon Institute of Business Studies in Johannesburg, from where he graduated in 2016. Feeling the calling to teach again, he stayed on at the institute to lecture in business studies.

### How to turn an organisation around

In 2017, the South African Heritage Resources Agency asked Thomas to take up the role of acting CEO. His main goal was to stabilise the entity after the CEO had been suspended, Thomas tells me as we sit in one of the meeting rooms at the institute's campus.

'The organisation had become dysfunctional, with management

splitting into different camps and a culture of mistrust brewing. Its performance suffered as a result and my first task was to rally the employees to work together.'

As a team they managed to steer the entity in the right direction and it achieved a clean audit for the first time in years. 'The employees began to feel happy, motivated and supported as opposed to hurt and confused. What I did was to sell the vision of what we could achieve and to develop a road map detailing the "when" and the "how" of achieving our goals. That clarity gave them direction. I could not have done it alone.'

It was also crucial for him to get the executive committee working again. 'I sat with them, and we went through the weaknesses and strengths of the organisation and determined what needed to be done. This created a sense of collective decision-making. It was important for me to do that, because as an interim CEO, I understood that my function was to empower the leadership so that there would be continuity once I left. In this regard, I delegated as much responsibility as possible, even to those who felt ill-equipped to handle what I threw at them.'

Thomas says he leads teams through 'healthy and robust engagements' and that he makes the time to get to know the people he works with on both a professional and a personal level. 'Given the changes we had to implement, I had to demand hard work and set strict targets. Furthermore, we ensured that we had a good relationship with the board and involved them in what we were doing through regular reporting.'

He was introduced to the aviation industry when he was approached in early 2018 to take up the position of interim CEO of Air Traffic and Navigation Services. The organisation went through a very turbulent time (pun unintended): it was not performing and a culture of fear reigned in the organisation, with many employees suspecting that their phones were being tapped by management.

Thomas managed to turn around the company and it went from achieving 50% of its key performance indicators to surpassing 85%.

He gave the executives a voice and told them he was always available if they needed help. Central to the turnaround was pulling the procurement process into the subcommittees of the company leadership and ensuring that due process was followed. He also streamlined the recruitment procedures.

'When everything is done according to the right processes and by following policies, people gain confidence in the leadership as it removes the suspicion that there is favouritism in the company. You should also create an environment where employees feel that they are allowed to make mistakes and that there is collaboration in steadying the ship. I made it clear that making mistakes should be viewed as part of the learning process and this brought a sense of calm and belonging that resulted in the company achieving its targets.'

### Juggling many things at once

Just as Thomas's stint at Air Traffic and Navigation Services came to an end, he was approached by a board member of SAA to take on the role as interim CEO as the airline transitioned from business rescue to finding a strategic equity partner.

'At the time I was very busy and thought the only way I could help her was by recommending the right person for the job. It wasn't an attractive proposition given the reputation of the airline and the well-documented challenges it faced. But she was quite insistent and I thought it wouldn't hurt to have a meeting with the board to get a better understanding of what the job would require.

'On meeting the board, I got the sense that they had the right intentions and were eager to rescue the jobs that would be lost should the airline be liquidated. We spent a good two hours during which we exchanged ideas and my questions were answered. After a follow-up meeting, I was convinced to join the company to spearhead their strategy for rebuilding the company.'

Thomas was formally appointed interim CEO of the airline in April 2021. He was tasked with creating a business case to restart the airline, which included completing a due diligence process and implementing compliance procedures. He faced many problems, including that financial statements had not been published since 2018. The most pressing issue was that the pilots were locked out due to a strike. The company also had to announce when the airline would take to the skies again after being grounded for many months.

I am curious to know how he manages to juggle running a national carrier with continuing to lecture. He explains that the good thing about the business institute is that its lecturing dates are scheduled early in the year, so he can block out that time. In addition, lecturers needn't be at the institute full time, but can come in for classes and then leave again.

'We are also encouraged to do consulting work so that we remain connected to the business world. I have a programme and an allocated number of hours that enable me to determine how much time I can spend on other work and my consulting company, Finequity Advisory, which I founded in 2013.'

Finequity Advisory does deal-making and has fewer than five employees. Thomas says they like to keep it lean because the services they offer (valuations, deal structuring and mergers) require 'a small group of highly trained thinkers'.

His lecturing position also allows Thomas to take up non-executive roles. 'I have a lot of things to do and it helps to schedule everything and to keep time. My first board role was in 2010 and so I have over a decade's experience at that level. Over time, I have learnt to categorise what's important and what isn't and have become more efficient. Of course, you must be organised!'

His secret weapon is to empower company executives quickly and to get them to take on more responsibilities. 'As a CEO you should never do more than you are supposed to, otherwise you will become overwhelmed. But at the same time, you must accept that a CEO's job is not about sitting on the beach and earning a fat pay cheque; you must be prepared to put in long hours if you are to meet the expectations of shareholders.'

Thomas has yet to serve on the board of a listed entity, but he finds boards in the private sector to be a closed network and directors tend to stay for a very long time. His niche appears to be acting in interim CEO roles because he has a track record of successfully turning around struggling entities. In such situations, boards require someone who is available immediately and is happy to serve in the position for a short period.

'I don't want a permanent position because that would pull me away from my passion of lecturing. I love the flexibility and interestingly, I do not go looking for these roles, I am always approached.

'If I had taken up the [permanent] SAA role, this interview would not be happening, because I would not have an hour to spare and I would struggle to drop off my kids at school, which is something I look forward to every morning. I'm also pursuing a PhD, which requires a lot of time for research. I wouldn't take up a permanent position – unless the pay is really too good to turn down.'

### Getting SAA to fly again

During his first month at SAA, Thomas had to spend a lot of time with the business rescue practitioner to understand the plan for saving the airline. Determining the restart date was not easy, because decisions like those require approval of not only the board but also the shareholder, who is represented by the relevant government minister.

A further complication was that SAA could not announce a restart date without pilots, who had been on strike for almost a year because of wage demands and talk of job cuts. The key thing was to get them to agree to return to work. Even then they could not simply jump into the aircraft and fly; they had to be reintegrated and start with simulations.

Thomas went to Cape Town to meet with the pilots and understand their demands. They were very disappointed with the government and took hard positions. 'I wanted to start on a clean slate and not get caught up in the shenanigans of the past,' Thomas recalls. 'Still, they were adamant that they wanted more money, which we simply did not have. The prolonged strike meant that many were on the verge of losing their cars and houses.

'We went back and forth and at times it got ugly, with the pilots calling me and the rest of the board all kinds of names. Eventually, we reached out to the pilots individually and made offers of back pay to ease their financial pressure and retrenched those who were not willing to return to enable them to access their pensions.'

Most of the pilots returned and SAA could then apply for their airport operating certificate. However, this wasn't simply a matter of filing a renewal notice – the airline had significant findings against it after the departure of quality control personnel, many of whom left in the months following the airline's wings being clipped in December 2019. Management put measures in place to address the findings and eventually the certificate was granted in May 2021.

'Many people believed that SAA was dead and I had to go on TV the following months to get the word out that we would be returning,' Thomas says. 'Another issue we faced was getting the aircraft back from the lessors, who had seized them when we went into business rescue at the onset of the COVID pandemic.'

Their next step was to assess which routes were the most profitable, and according to Thomas there were a few surprises. Whereas the Johannesburg–Cape Town route is possibly the busiest route on the continent, it is not very profitable, he explains.

The team therefore had to think beyond domestic routes and go international. SAA had a monopoly when it came to flights between Johannesburg and Accra and also Johannesburg and Lagos, so these were top of the list when the airline restarted in September. Unfortunately, there was not enough revenue from business travel at the time, but people were becoming tired of being locked up in their houses and as a consequence tourism started picking up.

Things were looking up. But then, in December 2021, the Omicron variant of the coronavirus that causes COVID-19 virus hit. Nigeria took the same stance as the UK and blacklisted South Africa, which dampened anticipated high revenues over the Christmas period. In looking at other ways to boost cash flow, SAA reopened the Johannesburg–Cape Town route. They realised this would be a good network enabler as someone who was flying from Accra to Cape Town could then book one ticket.

It took a while for the public to realise SAA was flying again because the company didn't have the budget to go on an advertising spree and had to rely on public relations and word of mouth. 'We also had a massive database of our voyager loyalty programme, so we could send emails to reach out to customers.

'By the time Omicron struck, we had some of our customers stuck in Mauritius as borders closed again. We had to pause Mauritius and also other routes because of the pandemic and also stiff competition from Comair. They were very aggressive, but I argued at the time that it would not be sustainable because an airline simply cannot meet it costs if it flies 40 people on an aircraft that should carry 160.'

Thomas points out that an aggressive strategy also leads to issues around reliability and consistency, which he was adamant they had to avoid. Besides Comair, FlySafair (one of the country's low-cost airlines) launched a price war by introducing sales campaigns that sold tickets for a giveaway R10.

'Our view was that we were serving a different customer base, namely businesspeople who wished to fly in comfort. Besides, the airline industry was in survival mode rather than growth; you cannot force growth to happen in a market that does not allow it. By making sound decisions on which routes to operate, we managed to improve the cash flow of SAA tremendously and by early 2022 we had stopped burning cash.'

### Be bold

Thomas believes that leadership is about managing relationships, especially in a complex environment such as a state-owned entity. You need good relationships with government, employees and the different unions and you should also foster an effective executive committee and engage the media appropriately.

Leaders should be bold and smart in their decision-making, he says. As CEO, you have to make key decisions, even if people oppose it. And when you have to make an unpopular call, be sure to do it for clear reasons, advises Thomas.

A good example is the Johannesburg–Durban route, which the government advocated for vigorously during the December 2021 holidays. Thomas had to put his foot down and say no – a very bold thing to do given that the government is SAA's main shareholder. Although the route made sense politically, it did not make sense commercially because it operated at a loss.

Another example that required brave decision-making was the business rescue of SAA's subsidiary, Mango Airlines. The unions had positioned themselves to handle the process, but SAA had to take them on and insist that it would be dealt with by the board.

'I was vilified in the media for this stance, but it's okay; I didn't take up the job at SAA to make friends,' Thomas says. 'I was there to make tough decisions, another of which was to incur the costs [of] fetching our stranded customers in Mauritius. As soon as borders were closed, I made a video and posted it online to let them know we were working to bring them home. That was important because SAA desperately needed to restore its reputation as a reliable airline that will serve customer interests despite documented financial challenges.'

In April 2022, Thomas handed over the reins to John Lamola, who was appointed CEO after a long search for the right candidate. He is back to running his advisory firm and teaching business students, but it is likely not to be long before he is approached by the next entity in dire need of a CEO-on-call to help save their business.

DiDATA & TOURVEST's **Sean Joubert**
*(Photo: Annith Botha)*

# SEAN JOUBERT

*Taking business personally*

'You can't put a square peg in a round hole.
CEOs do well when they are placed in positions
that are aligned to their core strengths.'

Sean Joubert is the kind of guy you could talk to for hours over a few beers. A fast talker, he makes his point with raw, honest wit and always has a few good stories to tell.

He was born in Johannesburg 56 years ago and grew up in a family of three children who all attended the same government school in Northcliff. Sean's rugby prowess earned him a scholarship to Rand Afrikaans University (today University of Johannesburg) where he completed his accounting studies.

After graduating with an honours degree in 1989, Sean secured an articles contract at Coopers & Lybrand (today PwC) and progressed to audit manager at the firm. In 1995, he joined the construction company WBHO as a financial accountant, but soon realised construction was not for him. So, when an opportunity came up to join Dimension Data (DiData for short) as a finance manager six months down the line, he did not hesitate.

He rose through the ranks at DiData and was appointed CEO of the South African business in 2011. He held this position for five years before resigning in 2016 'to look for something different'.

Given that he had been CEO of a company that traded IT, I was quite surprised to learn that Sean is not a big fan of technology. He was reluctant to have our interview online and needed his personal assistant to help him set it up and place the computer camera correctly.

'I have a love-hate relationship with technology,' he admits. 'In fact, IT scares me because I'm a bit of a traditionalist. People laugh at me because of that. But don't get me wrong: I enjoyed working with the people at Dimension Data. It was an innovative, creative and go-getter type of organisation. That said, I didn't spend my spare time reading about Bill Gates or Steve Jobs or the next big solution or trend. I don't hate technology; I just prefer to be social and to exist as a human being outside of machines.'

### Joining Tourvest

'In 2016, I sent my CV out to a couple of head-hunters with the instruction to call me if something really different [from a position in IT] came up. Sure, DiData was a dynamic environment where you got to work hard and play hard. But I wanted something in another industry. Then an agent informed me that Tommy Edmond, CEO at Tourvest, was retiring.'

For Sean it seemed like a dream job because of his love of travel, recreational activities and an obsession with sport, particularly rugby. Joining a company whose primary purpose was selling enjoyment promised to transform him from a tech trader to a merchant of merriment.

In January 2018 he was appointed group CEO of Tourvest – and he hasn't looked back one day. Sean firmly believes that he makes a better CEO when he is passionate about a business.

'My biggest strength is probably one of my biggest weaknesses. I take things quite personally, because for me things are personal. If something is close to one's heart, it drives innovation and clearer decision-making. If you are the CEO of a company that is close to your value system, your purpose in life or the things you find interesting, you will definitely be more effective as a leader.'

His first two years leading the group were phenomenal. But then the

COVID-19 pandemic struck. The group is a broad business across different geographies and 'a really great team'. Although the pandemic hit the travel and hospitality industry particularly hard, Sean wouldn't trade the experience for anything. 'It brought our team together and helped foster respect for one another,' he reflects.

Before COVID-19, the group had hundreds of million rand in overhead base per month, but during the first month of lockdown, they only invoiced R1 million. Things looked gloomy for a long time as revenues sat at only about 10%–15% of their pre-COVID-19 numbers. But even though the technology industry did relatively better, Sean did not for one minute wish that he was back in that space.

'You have to take what life throws your way and I have learnt a lot,' he reflects. 'I have grown and developed resilience and determination to handle any corporate crisis. That will always stand me in good stead. In any case, I am not one to overstay my welcome and it was time for me to move on from DiData.'

During the pandemic, Sean fell back on a meeting he once had with Springbok coach Jacques Nienaber during which they discussed parallels between their roles. On the journey to winning the Rugby World Cup in 2019, the Springboks' leadership told the team to ignore the weight of what felt like the whole African continent on their shoulders and instead to focus simply on winning the next game. Sean realised to get Tourvest through the COVID-19 crisis the company need this approach to winning.

As a consequence, the management team embraced the fact that they were the only ones who could save the company. 'This informed every single decision we took,' Sean explains. 'Like the Springbok team, we focused on the main thing: for the players it was to win games; for us it was to save the company. Whether it was salary sacrifices, deferring incentive schemes or cost cutting – the main thing was for us to go home and look ourselves in the mirror and say the team decision was to save the company.'

Tourvest's management team rose to the challenge thanks to the culture of the organisation, which is one of ownership, accountability and transparency. According to Sean, each member of the management team ran their division as if it was their own. So, when it came to spending money, they would ask themselves if they would spend that money if they owned the company. They also needed to believe in one another, just like a rugby player who passes the ball trusts his fellow players to catch it.

Sean's analogy also extends to football teams (he is a big Liverpool fan). When football teams sustain a string of losses, fans and commentators often demand that the coach be fired. The decision then has to be whether you submit and drop the coach, or ignore the noise and continue to support the coach in his strategy.

'Coaches have a much better chance of turning things around if you back them. United you stand, divided you fall. That is what got us through the crisis. It is amazing that despite the challenges, the entire core leadership team stuck with the company when they could have easily jumped ship.

'We succeeded because we did not lose the change room. Our culture of unity saved the day, together with good relationships with banks and landlords.'

### Wearing his heart on his sleeve

Sean wants to sell something he believes in. 'I'm not the only one who is thriving – the entire leadership team is doing extremely well,' he says. 'And why wouldn't we be? It's a sexy business, quite different from a tech firm. Whether it is retail shops, restaurants or lodges, we have a pool of really cool stuff. The purpose of our portfolio of 60 different businesses is to create happy experiences. We have value-based leadership where the management is closely aligned to the values of the organisation and that brings out the best in them.'

Sean is proof that leadership skills are largely transferable from one industry to another. 'As long as the company you move to isn't out of this world – like NASA [space agency]!' he jokes. 'It took me less than a year to feel I knew enough about this industry to have a grip on it. A good leader is a fast learner – and should also be teachable.

'It's also crucial that your principles are aligned with that of the organisation. I wear my heart on my sleeve, which means I am transparent and honest, and call it like I see it. So, people know where they stand with me.'

Strong leadership is about effective communication, Sean says. It requires creating a clear vision, reinforcing it and constant communication about it. It is about giving direction to the organisation and getting employees to buy into your vision so that it can be executed. Actions have to be measurable so that employees can be held accountable. Sean believes these are fundamentals for any CEO, regardless of the industry they are in.

To scale the heights of corporate leadership, it helps to have a solid foundation based on a qualification in a relevant discipline, such as accounting, law or engineering. According to Sean, degrees as such teach you how to solve problems and handle stress, as they typically come with difficult exams and much pressure.

However, to run an organisation requires a broad range of skills that go beyond what you learnt in university, Sean says. For one, you need to be able to leave your comfort zone and think outside the box. It also requires people skills, because an organisation is made up of many different kinds of individuals, and a good leader must learn to deal with all of them.

Being able to influence people is another important skill in a leader toolset, says Sean. Trust, credibility and integrity are therefore key, because people need to know that 'you say what you mean and mean what you say'.

'CEOs also do well when they are in a business whose specific needs are aligned to their strengths,' Sean observes. 'You can't put a square peg in a round hole. For example, you can't put a CEO who struggles to disappoint people in a company looking for a turnaround strategy. In such a position the person would be unable to restructure the company or retrench people because they'd hate to be the bearer of bad news.'

Sean surrounds himself with very capable colleagues because he believes leaders' biggest problem is the humility to accept that they do not know it all. 'Such leaders do not surround themselves with people who can augment, complement and challenge them.

'I am not afraid to sit in a room with someone who is smarter than me. I understand that I don't know everything and therefore I put an effort into building a diverse team with different competencies and knowledge. I help them grow and I coach them.'

### Making Tourvest more resilient

Today, Tourvest's revenue is approximately 70% of their pre-pandemic invoicing and the business has returned to profitability. The corporate travel business recently billed its highest amount of revenue in the history of the company.

Sean gets annoyed by terms such as 'new normal' and 'post-pandemic era'. He recalls having robust discussions with board members and shareholders about the future of the business after the pandemic. They would refer to images of people at a restaurant in Paris having a meal with glass panels around each diner as how they expected life would be like after COVID-19.

'I argued strongly that such a scenario was not sustainable. Many of us in this industry believed the things we were witnessing during the pandemic were temporary. People were always going to go to restaurants, travel on planes, stay in hotels and jump off bridges. So COVID-19 didn't impact the lifestyles of our customer. However, what it did teach us is that our business model is very vulnerable.'

Businesses like Tourvest are vulnerable to the impacts of macroeconomic factors such as acts of terrorism, pandemics and wars, as well as the ways in which governments react to them. In Sean's view, lockdowns did little in fighting the pandemic.

To make their business more resilient, Tourvest is now focused on diversifying operations to multiple geographies and in different segments. The group is also developing domestic tourism products, which proved to be a solid income-earner during lockdowns.

Sean admits to being something of a socialist and being passionate about creating an equal society. He constantly worries about how those who did not have the privileged background he had can be uplifted. 'People find this surprising because they expect a CEO to be obsessed with profits and shareholder value. I am more concerned about closing the gap between the rich and poor in South Africa.'

Sean defines success as being content with what you have achieved. 'For some it is to have a job that lets them travel from country to country. Some want to become billionaires. And for others, like my daughter Jessica, it is to work with children in disadvantaged rural communities. To be successful is to do something that gets you out of bed in the morning.'

# POLO LETEKA

*A 'dragon' with a teachable spirit*

'Leadership starts with self-leadership:
to be a good leader you should first have a vision for yourself.'

Polo Leteka, founder and chairman of IDF Capital, is a dragon in more ways than one. In a very literal sense, she was one of the five power women on the South African franchise of *Dragons' Den*. In a more figurative sense, she has the fire of a dragon in her when it comes to gender issues and putting women first.

On the TV show, which ran in 2014, aspiring entrepreneurs pitched their business ideas to the quintet of 'dragons', who would scrutinise their idea before deciding who they wanted to invest in.

'When I was first approached to take part in the show, I declined. "I'm an accountant, not an actor", I thought,' Polo recalls. But she reconsidered after a while.

The clincher was when she learnt that all the other dragons were men. 'I thought it was important to bring in a female perspective and it would also be educational for our people to understand about entrepreneurship. I wanted a girl in rural KwaZulu-Natal watching the show to learn something and hopefully see what she can become, to know that she too can be a dragon one day, or that she could pitch a business idea and get investment from a venture capitalist.'

Polo was a fan of the original British show and so she immediately understood what was required. 'It was more than just good TV. In fact, we recently exited one of the transactions, namely Bloomable

IDF CAPITAL's **Polo Leteka**
*(Photo: Bridget Corke Photography)*

[formerly SA Florist] at a decent return. IDF also invested in others, although they sadly did not perform so well.'

Other than identifying feasible projects, she had a lot of fun on the show – some business ideas were so ridiculous she bent over with laughter. Even after the show had ended, people would still walk up to her in a mall or at a garage to pitch their ideas.

### Investing in women

In founding IDF Capital in March 2008, Polo's challenge was to unlock what she knew in her heart to be true: that women have tremendous power to bring about change. IDF Capital invests in entrepreneurial small and medium enterprises, particularly those that are led by women.

The company is set on convincing critics that women are an asset class and that diverse teams can be depended on to deliver good returns. 'We live in a patriarchal society, so women are often not welcome in investment spaces, which are often male dominated,' Polo explains. 'Our structures and institutions serve men more than women. In many cultures, some women are not even comfortable speaking to men. Globally, gender prejudice is an intangible phenomenon and one that cannot be easily addressed. This is why we have been very intentional about what we are doing.

'The structural issues around prejudice mostly concern attitudes. For example, when a woman approaches a fund manager, she will typically be speaking to a man. The man would probably deny her funding, either because he doesn't believe in her capability as a woman or because he struggles to understand the problem she is trying to solve. It is a significant problem when you consider that women make up more than 50% of the world population yet they're excluded from certain services and products because conventional funders do not consider their opportunities to be commercially viable.'

Research suggests that women have traits that are generally attributed to strong leaders. They are compassionate and listen with the intention to truly understand, instead of merely responding. Good leaders are intuitive and are said to plan; they don't just do things on a whim.

'From that perspective, an argument can be made that women tend to be better entrepreneurs than men,' Polo says. 'Entrepreneurs who do well are those who are willing to listen and take advice. In a high-level study of our portfolio, we found that women outperformed men.'

When Polo started her business in 2008, they were the only female investment fund managers that were listed by the Southern Africa Venture Capital and Private Equity Association. Today the association indicates that the proportion of female fund managers has increased to 30%. These days funders with deep pockets are approaching the IDF because of their specific focus.

'We are proud to have had a role in increasing the amount of money that is invested in women,' Polo says. 'According to statistics from the African Development Bank some time ago, even though more than 40% of small and medium-sized businesses on the continent are run by women, less than 2% of funding goes to them. We are starting to see this changing and I look forward to the day we hit 50%.'

### *Know your strengths and weaknesses*

When I ask her about her advice for entrepreneurs, Polo says she would encourage them to have a 'teachable spirit'. They must accept that simply because they came up with an idea doesn't mean that they are the best person to execute it. Many people do not even have the relevant skills to implement their ideas.

'Be thirsty for knowledge,' she advises. 'When I started my business, I used to invite strategically selected people to lunch. I'd write notes and ask lots of questions as we ate. People have really good information to share, which you won't find in a textbook. You need to have the humility to accept that you have limited knowledge; nobody knows everything. And the great thing about advice is that you don't have to take all of it. Take what makes sense to you at the time.'

She also believes you should be curious and not be afraid to fail. She has learnt that apart from gathering sufficient information to start a project, you should expect to make mistakes – but that they are there to learn from. Playing safe will not get you very far.

'When we started this business, we would finance anything – transport, manufacturing, agriculture. But we didn't invest in technology businesses because we found it a very specialised space,' Polo recalls. 'As accountants, we lacked that tech mindset. But we realised that tech start-ups are disrupting traditional business models and we eventually took the plunge. So we decided that when someone comes to us with an app or web-based platform but isn't able to show it to us yet, we could put in a small amount – like R100 000 – in and then keep increasing our investment as the product actualised. Today, we run a technology accelerator – I'M IN – and other fund managers even seek advice from us when evaluating tech proposals.'

IDF Capital has made several successful investments, including in SweepSouth, EMGuidance, MortgageMarket, Netcampus, Lula Loop and Jetstream. The company manages funds from investors (who are looking for a commercial return), but in doing so they are intentional about ensuring that women are the biggest benefactors of the money they deploy. With their goal being to support women as entrepreneurs, employees or consumers, the fund always considers how the money they deploy can have a multiplier effect in the communities where they operate.

IDF also invests in male-owned businesses, but in those cases they ensure that they drive transformation in areas such as the composition of the board, leadership structure and staff complement. They also look at who buys the products and services and the channels that are used for distribution.

'A company need not tick all the boxes for us to invest,' Polo explains. 'We identify areas where we can help. Let's say there is an agro-processing business that buys 80% from men and 20% from women. We would look at how we can improve farming among women so that the company can buy more of their produce. We develop a transformation strategy with a view to making it gender diverse across the value chain by the time we exit the investment.'

### 'Intelligent capital'

When starting to review a proposal, IDF Capital uses a financial model to determine the desired return they're looking for. Because they manage private equity funds, they must exceed investor requirements. Often they are part of the process to help a business achieve high returns.

'We ask ourselves: What are the things we must unlock for this business to grow its sales and improve its efficiencies so that we can increase profitability? For example, our investment thesis might say that a business is selling $1 million and if we do four specific things it could get to $10 million in five years' time. So, we must understand what the four value levers are to get to that target. It could entail improving systems, bringing in the right people or providing certain resources.'

Polo became an entrepreneur because she understood the important role that financial capital plays. She recalls how someone called what IDF does 'intelligent capital' because the company brings not only money to the table but also the brains within the establishment. 'It's a totally different approach from that of financial institutions that grant only loans to companies and then pull back, hoping for a good outcome.'

Polo believes in the potential of Africans to rise above the challenges that have bedevilled the continent. She wants to help unlock Africa's potential for the benefit of all its people and not just half of them. IDF Capital can be a catalyst in that process, she says.

IDF also considers transformation, because potential partners will pay a premium to invest in a company that has the right environmental, social and corporate governance framework. Funders also rate gender and racial diversity highly because research shows that diverse teams produce much better returns.

To oversee these interventions, Polo sits on the boards of the companies that IDF Capital has invested in and has monthly report-back meetings with them. This helps her to understand their challenges and to identify the kind of support they need, including bringing in external expertise when necessary. As investors, IDF therefore not only offers strategic thinking, but also enables a company to tap into their broad business network.

Polo is often approached by banks and other listed companies to sit on their boards, but she mostly declines because these roles are very time consuming. She considers sitting on a board to be a serious fiduciary responsibility, which should not be taken lightly. One needs to understand the company intricately and read the board pack carefully before attending meetings.

Her plate is already full given that she spends a lot of time with the management of IDF's investees, chairs the Early Care Foundation and is president of the Association of Black Securities and Investment Professionals.

### Living by a to-do list

Polo believes leadership starts with self-leadership: to be a good leader you should first have a vision for yourself. You will encounter many obstacles – and of different kinds – along your way and without a clear vision, a quest can easily be abandoned.

'When times get tough, I remind myself that my mission is possible and I am the person to achieve it because I am the owner of my vision. Linked to this is perseverance, because moments of discouragement will come; I need to have a source of energy to rely on during dark times.

'I pray every morning, because I don't know what problems I'll have to face during the day. I encourage others to do whatever works for them, whether it's exercise, meditation or yoga. But have something that feeds your spirit when you encounter challenges.'

According to Polo a good leader is also disciplined. She thrives on routine and regularly checks and updates the to-do list on her phone. Often unforeseen things disrupt her plans, but she religiously goes back to her list to complete outstanding tasks, even if it means dedicating a couple of hours outside work time to get them done. And because she hates working on weekends, she does her best to get her list done during the week.

It is diligence, discipline and dedication – and a very organised to-do list – that makes this dragon an increasingly dominant force in the world of investment.

DIS-CHEM's **Rui Morais**
*(Photo: Courtesy of Dis-Chem)*

# RUI MORAIS

*Leading by listening*

'When a customer walks down our aisles, there must always be
something that excites them. To do that, you need to go to the ground level
and experience things the way the customer is experiencing them.'

Few occasions test a man's nerves more than having to pace up and
down a cold and dim hospital corridor waiting for his first child to be
born. It gets worse when the doctor eventually emerges to advise that
the child is stuck in the birth canal.

In 2017 Rui Morais felt fear grip him like a wrench when his wife,
Roxanne, went into labour. Thankfully, their daughter Olivia was safely
delivered, but it gave the current CFO and CEO designate of the pharmacy chain Dis-Chem first-hand knowledge of the importance of proper
healthcare.

He met Roxanne in 2002, when they were both first-year students
at Rand Afrikaans University (today the University of Johannesburg).
Their study fields couldn't be more different – Rui taking up accounting while Roxanne was studying industrial psychology.

Rui matriculated at the age of 17 and in 1995, by the age of 21 had
an honours degree in his pocket. He joined EY for articles a year later,
where he was assigned to the retail audit division. One of his first audit
assignments was for Dis-Chem Pharmacies and he soon got to meet
the founders of the company, Ivan and Lynette Saltzman.

He had a regular auditor–client relationship with the couple for
several years until the Dis-Chem management team decided to transition to the SAP software system to run their operations. 'SAP is

quite a robust and rigid system created by a German software firm and moving over to the platform presented Dis-Chem with some challenges given that the business has an entrepreneurial culture. Fitting it to an off-the-shelf, standard system was not easy.'

Rui impressed Ivan with his ideas around how to address these issues. 'That is where the conversation began of me joining the business. I liked his thought processes and the excellent group of partners who had been working with him for a long time already.'

He joined the company's finance department in 2011. 'When I walked into Dis-Chem, I was impressed with the way they had differentiated themselves from their competitors as a retail brand and the novelty of the items they stocked.'

### Business talk

Rui is thankful for studying accounting and believes it has enabled him to move up the corporate ladder quickly. 'Finance is the consequence of all commercial decisions,' he says. 'Having financial knowledge enables you to participate in discussions that are relevant to business. When you're young, you don't have the experience from years of service, so studying something finance related offers a shortcut to senior positions. Experience differentiates operational people, while financial personnel depend on their academic knowledge to get a head start on understanding the mechanics of the business.'

In Dis-Chem, he has found a company that aligns with his personality and aspirations, since he has an entrepreneurial nature that thrives in a fast-growing company. The entity was founded in 1978 when the Saltzmans were newly qualified pharmacists. They introduced the concept of a discount pharmacy with product categories not previously offered in other South African stores.

In March 2022, Dis-Chem launched their own health insurance. 'The company is joining the rest of the private sector in ensuring that people who cannot rely on the state for healthcare are catered for,' Rui says. 'This is a mission that is close to my heart. I have the opportunity of being part of the move towards digital healthcare and a changing healthcare market. We have become more than just a retail pharmacy; our priority is to become a fully fledged health management organisation.'

In an interview with *Financial Mail* in 2020, Rui was asked what he would do or change if he became president. His answer was that he would try to extract more out of the private sector. 'We have world-class businesses that have solved complex solutions, and we could use that … for South Africa. We should all be, in some way or form, contributing to a better SA.'

Rui was appointed the pharmacy chain's CFO in 2012 and one of his most difficult assignments was listing the company on the Johannesburg Stock Exchange four years later. 'Dealing with the institutional investors and the pressures that they create can lead to many difficult moments,' he states. 'They have very high expectations, but I realised you cannot please everyone; that is the nature of the market.

'Being on a listed exchange means that there is often high liquidity, so people can invest in a stock one day and if they don't like the direction it is headed in, they sell. When we first listed, we were quite worried about disappointing people, but we have since come to understand that we have to believe in the story we are writing and accept that not everyone is going to walk with you on that journey.'

Being part of the evolution of the brand has been a great high for Rui. He joined the group when they had less than 20 stores, and now they have over 290 outlets, following the acquisition of Baby City and Medicare Health.

### Leaders who listen

Rui had a significant role in this growth trajectory and in mid-2021 it was announced that he would be taking over as CEO when Ivan retired. Even though he was only 37 at the time, Rui says he wasn't daunted by the task of being CEO of a listed entity with a turnover of R26 billion, because he felt he had the necessary support. 'I have always been younger than others at my level ... I've come to terms with the fact that age need not influence the outcome of what you are trying to do. At Dis-Chem the major shareholders have invested a lot of time to ensure that I have the necessary exposure.'

In Rui's opinion one of the key qualities a CEO should have is the ability to listen. 'Ivan always surprised me. Despite how successful he was and the fact that he was much more knowledgeable than others in the business, he truly listened to people's ideas, even someone like me when I was just 26 with very little commercial experience.'

Ivan inculcated a family culture in the company, particularly at management level where everyone is given a platform to contribute to the strategic intent.

Rui believes a high emotional intelligence outweighs a theoretical understanding of management principles. A good leader identifies people with an inherent ability to influence others and gives them the opportunity to lead. This is regardless of their age, race or gender. In this regard, Rui tries to be as inclusive as possible.

'Fairness, openness and transparency are important values of a leader. If you demonstrate these, you'll be able to manage the difficult times and take advantage of the good times. You need to understand the different personalities on your team and you have to know what motivates them, what influences them and also what is going on in their personal lives.

'A leader is placed in a certain position to make key decisions and must be held accountable for those decisions. Still, that does not mean that they should discount the views of those who disagree with them. Good leadership also entails being able to rationalise a decision to your team and get their buy-in so that everyone pulls together in the chosen direction.'

## *Leaving a legacy*

Part of Dis-Chem's success has come from benchmarking its strategy against global peers. The company is effectively going down the same road as the British and American markets, where independent pharmacies are consolidating their businesses to form merged entities rather than remain independent of big groups. Dis-Chem is incorporating those principles and making them relevant to the South African market.

The next thing is making sure the executive team is on the same page. When an entity grows as fast as they have in the last 10 years, it's crucial that employees understand the company strategy and what the business priorities are. With so many things going on, key aspects of the business must be in order, and you can't focus too intensely on the small things, says Rui.

'This includes keeping the core of the brand intact and service levels high when acquiring other entities. We must ensure that when a customer walks down our aisles, there will always be something that excites them. To do that you need to go to the ground level and experience things the way the customer is experiencing them.

'In a listed environment, where you face constant pressure to manage costs, it's easy to forget the customer. But you must be prepared to suffer losses in one or two years as you pursue long-term gain, and have the confidence to make those decisions even under the pressures of the investment community. Gauging the customer experience ensures that there is no disconnect between strategy and execution.'

The journey with Dis-Chem has led to many long nights and weekends in the office for Rui, who says he would love to see the company become the biggest retail pharmacy in South Africa. While his career is fulfilling and challenging, family life is equally important to him. Four years after Olivia was born, he and Roxanne had another daughter, Rafaela, which means 'God is our healer'.

'I wish for my girls grow up in a stable, loving environment like the one my brother and I grew up in. I hope to raise them to understand the dynamics of South Africa and the many opportunities this country has. My life's motto is to try and leave the world in a better state than I found it; I hope to instil the same yearning in my kids.'

# ERIK SMUTS

*The curious CEO with a can-do attitude*

'No matter how much experience you have – if
employees don't trust you, they won't respect you.'

Nampak CEO Erik Smuts is always up for a challenge – whether in life or in business. He is the kind of person who is intrigued by the unknown, instead of shying away from it.

After he completed his honours degree at the University of Pretoria in 1993, he joined Deloitte for his three years of articles. When the opportunity for a year's secondment came around, he didn't choose a familiar environment like the UK or US; instead he chose to join the Budapest office in Hungary to do computer auditing. Erik thought it would be an adventure because Communism had fallen in Eastern Europe just a few years before and the region was opening up to the rest of the world.

On a personal front, Erik also challenges himself and likes to ponder the many unanswered questions of life. In recent times, he has read up on theoretical physics. He doesn't have a formal background in science, but he is fascinated by notions such as the speed of light and cosmology. He got into it during moments of professional crises when he was looking for intellectual stimulation unrelated to his line of work.

Back to his time in Hungary. He faced a lot of down time, because he needed a translator to scrutinise documents and there wasn't always one available. Not feeling productive enough, Erik started shopping around for a different job. It wasn't long before he got one at Nampak.

NAMPAK's **Erik Smuts**
*(Photo: Melissa Naidoo)*

'I've always been interested in business,' Erik says. 'This is what inspired me to pursue a CIMA [Chartered Institute of Management Accountants] qualification alongside my chartered accountant designation. With auditing you are merely commenting on other people's business; you're not in a position to own the results a company produced.'

Erik wanted in on the action. 'I joined Nampak as a project accountant in the beverage canning [Bevcan] division. My initial project was to oversee the implementation of the Hyperion software system and before long I was involved with inventory control and production planning.'

Working as an assistant for the sales and marketing director, Erik was later roped into negotiating terms with both suppliers and customers. That experience taught him that a proactive employee can structure his duties towards his skill set despite what his formal job description is.

In 2001, four years after he joined Nampak, he was appointed commercial director of the division, which allowed him to get experience in different parts of the business. Another four years later, he was appointed financial director of the division. He was responsible for its financial performance, although the financial reporting was handled exclusively by the financial manager. In 2009, he became the division's managing director and by 2020 took over as group CEO.

Erik believes accountants who want to lead companies must make the call to become generalists rather than specialists. They are similar to engineers, who are trained to apply common sense, an essential quality for leadership. Both professions require proficiency in mathematics, a discipline that can only be understood by applying logic, and leadership is all about logical decision-making in the search for solutions.

Accountants have an added advantage, though, because finance is the language of business. In his view, a finance qualification is therefore an accelerator for those harbouring ambitions of getting into the C-suite.

### Adapting to stay competitive

During the time he headed Bevcan, Erik saw an evolution in both the company and the industry. There was consolidation through mergers and industry changes arising from some players going out of business. There also were periods when there was little investment in the business, which led to the local industry becoming uncompetitive.

However, pressure from multinational clients meant the business had to become more competitive. Following the first democratic elections in 1994, the South African market opened up and companies like Nampak have had to re-invent themselves to survive. In this adapt-or-die scenario, Nampak adopted high-speed aluminium production systems as part of their strategy to stay profitable.

Cans have also been under threat from plastics, which are increasingly used to bottle soft drinks. Furthermore, glass became a popular alternative for the bottling of beers and other alcoholic products. To respond to these changes, Nampak turned to the export market to keep up volumes. They also embarked on a strong marketing campaign to promote the use of cans under the 'CAN DO!' slogan.

'In 2012, we set up a factory in Angola that was successful from the word go,' Erik says. 'We wanted to do the same thing in Nigeria, but because there was a newly built factory that suited our purposes, we decided to buy the premises instead. Both businesses started off well, but around 2014 the oil price collapsed and both countries faced economic collapse. Because of the currency crunch we struggled to repatriate funds and get sufficient foreign exchange to pay our suppliers.'

Although both businesses are efficient and profitable, Erik says the economic situation must improve before they can achieve greater profits. 'We are often asked if we would consider an exit. We would, yes, but at the right price. We must consider the returns against the risks of keeping the businesses going.'

Marketing by competitors such as Consol (which sells glass) has re-energised both can and glass products. Lately, however, there has been capacity shortages of both products and Nampak is struggling to satisfy demand in the market.

The alcohol bans during the COVID-19 pandemic resulted in a glass shortage because the furnaces had to keep going and churned out glass waste when they weren't allowed to produce beer bottles. In turn, this resulted in lost capacity and when the market reopened there was insufficient stock to satisfy demand. Since then, the market has exploded.

'Our businesses are affected by customer preferences. For example, today beer drinkers prefer the smaller, single-use bottles to returnable quarts. The smaller bottles and cans are in the same market, which has benefited us. There is a lingering perception that you can taste the metal when drinking from a can, but this is a false marketing narrative because all blind tests we have conducted prove otherwise. In fact, most test case respondents chose the sample in a can over the one in glass.

'Others think it's cooler to be seen holding a bottle than a can, but in terms of the taste, a can would definitely be better. Beer is affected by light, which is why they sell it in dark bottles. Regardless of how dark the bottle is, the light will still get through. Cans do not have that problem.'

## Building a culture of trust

In Erik's view it is critical for a leader to understand the business they are running and what their role is. He says managers easily get trapped in doing something that is not their job. Leaders should also know their limitations: Erik may be the CEO, but he would never want to be put on the production line because he isn't a can-maker. His job is to look at how things can be aligned and made easier for those who are the experts at their jobs.

You only have a certain number of hours a day and you simply cannot do everything, he says. Management is about aligning resources to leverage the skill of those you manage. If you do so, it will multiply the skill factor. In this regard, trust is key. 'It doesn't matter how much experience you have – if employees don't trust you, they won't respect you,' he says.

'In a business, employees need to feel like they trust their leaders and leaders need to feel that they trust their employees,' Erik states. 'As a leader, I don't have to micromanage employees when I trust them. This is what brings about a multiplication factor, because we end up allowing people to do their jobs without interruption. We only need to monitor from time to time and identify areas where they're falling short, and then we can give them the necessary support, which, in turn, will allow us to continue trusting them.'

Eric's viewpoint links to what Stephen Covey says in *The Speed of Trust* about the benefits of having trust in a business. For one, trust relationships lead to better communication because it is far easier to understand someone you trust – like friends who understand each other much faster than when strangers communicate. Trust also helps to lower costs because a company will have to spend less on marketing if they have a product their customers trust. Similarly, suppliers would not need to gather so much information from a customer to initiate a credit transaction if their relationship is built on trust.

'Beyond trust, integrity and honesty are also important,' Erik continues. 'These are the values that should inform the business strategy. A strategy needs to focus on alignment and should not be too complicated. It is crucial for employees to understand what the strategy is and how they can contribute towards its success.'

As part of their strategy, Nampak has four categories of intervention, based on risk and growth.

The first considers debt management, currently Nampak's biggest risk and which they are aiming to reduce. Secondly, their strategy aims to simplify the business portfolio and the processes within those businesses. Thirdly, they focus on optimisation, which entails improving how they use resources, streamlining throughput, lowering wastage and optimising procurement.

Nampak can't do much to differentiate itself with the ultimate product; they have to produce cans according to the customer's specifications. Their last category of intervention therefore centres on driving innovation in the production process by improving the quality of the product, lowering costs and ensuring seamless service delivery.

'All tasks centre around these four categories. Whenever a new project is presented, the first thing we do is to check what strategic category it fits into. In that way the entire business – from recruits to the most experienced workers – are aligned in terms of what we are aiming to achieve,' Erik explains.

### Focus on where you can make a difference

His first years as CEO weren't easy. The COVID-19 pandemic hit soon after he was appointed in the executive role and the group has increasingly needed to carry high debt levels. This means Nampak is constantly working to get their balance sheet in shape and it will take many years to achieve.

However, there have also been highlights in his career, like when they reshaped the beverage can industry in sub-Saharan Africa. 'We have been successful in the face of macro-economic challenges. Sadly, the bigger economic picture is out of our control and as a result we need to do some careful tap dancing given the risks in our constrained balance sheet.'

Erik knows not worrying about things beyond your control is easier said than done. 'Unfortunately, when investors see bad results, they don't care too much whether it's because of your actions or because of circumstances beyond your control. That causes stress. But ultimately you have to concentrate on the areas where you can in fact make a difference.'

Like the Bevcan slogan, Erik has a can-do attitude in everything he does. He is also an accomplished cyclist who has done mountain bike races across the world, including the Trans Andes, the Swiss Epic, the BC Bike Race in Canada and the Cape Epic. Level-headed and grounded yet curious to explore the unknown, he is always ready to cycle to the next hill to see what lies beyond.

# LEILA FOURIE

*Bringing a rock climber's mindset to business*

'Climbing has taught me that without risk, life is dull and colourless.
We need to seek out that which takes us out of our comfort zone
and gives us strength rather than safety.'

Leila Fourie, CEO of the Johannesburg Stock Exchange (JSE) grew up in Johannesburg in a family of 10. This taught her already from a young age to compromise and sacrifice. Many of her values stem from her upbringing and strong female role models in her family – her mother and her jeweller grandmother. From them she also learnt the importance of forgiveness, humility and determination.

Leila describes herself as a 'perpetual student', who, even as a child, showed a great love of reading. She shares a fond memory of a day when she speed read a book and then ran down a steep road to get to Parkhurst Library in time before it closed to get the next book in the series.

She completed her undergraduate studies at the Rand Afrikaans University (today University of Johannesburg) in 1987. She later also pursued a master's in financial economics at the same university, graduating in 2011. Her dissertation on procyclicality in the South African credit market, which focused on the lending patterns of banks through economic cycles, particularly during recessions that exacerbate economic crises, was chosen as the best study by the Economic Society of South Africa.

For her PhD thesis, which she completed in 2015, Leila created a

JSE & AUSTRALIA PAYMENTS NETWORK's **Leila Fourie**

*(Photo: Devin Lester)*

quantitative model to study the effect of contagion on countries' sovereign ratings. Her findings showed that the next source of economic contagion would come from China. It turned out to be prescient research: the COVID-19 pandemic thrust the world into a global health and economic crisis just a few years later.

'I don't think I'll ever stop learning, whether it's in the formal sphere or through reading and interacting with others. It's something close to my heart, which I have also tried to instil in my children,' Leila says. 'One of my favourite lessons from Microsoft CEO Satya Nadella teaches you that organisations should seek to change from being "those that know a lot to those that learn a lot". That is something I've tried to introduce at the JSE – a yearning for knowledge and an understanding that we don't have all the answers.'

With her background in economics, Leila worked for Accenture, Standard Bank and the JSE before moving to Australia in 2016 to take up the role of CEO of the Australian Payments Network. In 2019, she was approached to become the new CEO of the JSE. It was not an easy decision to return to the country of her birth because it meant leaving behind her family in Australia and working in a different time zone than them.

'I'm at the tail end of my career in executive employment, and I figured I should take up this opportunity before retiring to serve on different boards as a non-executive. I did not want to spend my life wondering whether I should have taken up the job and having regrets for not doing so. I also saw it as an opportunity to play a part in South African society given the compounding growth effect the JSE has in the economy.'

### Managing a stock exchange

Generally speaking, the JSE's business is performing well. The exchange is required to ensure that price formation still happens during times of crisis. This means that a price should be available to make trades of shares and technology and regulation should support the execution of such trades. This is particularly important during periods of high volumes such as when the market was bearish at the start of the COVID-19 pandemic.

Despite this crisis, the business has been resilient. The stock market has been affected by events such as South Africa's sovereign rating being downgraded to sub-investment grade and the recent Russia–Ukraine war, both of which created volatility in volumes and values. The JSE's job is to ensure that the system can handle these events, which it does through appropriate regulation and oversight and the right technology.

'We are the 19th largest exchange in the world,' says Leila. 'This means that we punch above our real economy weight given that we are the 36th largest economy by GDP. On the one hand, we offer individuals an opportunity for savings and on the other, the ability for companies to raise capital. The regulation, oversight and infrastructure we provide must be efficient to ensure that the price of the assets reflects the sentiment or intention of the investors.'

Of course, there have also been challenges, including disruptive system failures. However, these crises pale in comparison to the trauma caused by COVID-19. 'We experienced great loss – some staff members directly and some of their family members. The pain permeated the whole organisation. It was the most difficult challenge of my leadership career because we didn't have a playbook for this kind of situation.'

To steer the company to continued profitability, Leila has a leading role in crafting strategy. She believes a strategy is born from understanding the market and the needs that must be fulfilled.

It is also crucial to have a level of innovation and imagination. Success does not take a straight line, she says, meaning that organisations must be responsive and able to identify a future path. This may not be a sequential next step, Leila apprises. Furthermore, management should be aware of their strengths and weaknesses.

Leila reiterates her delight in the role her organisation plays in the broader society and says its impact on building markets has a ripple effect. 'Apart from having the opportunity to create enabling infra-structure and markets, the JSE can also help to build the economy and expand our markets ... When I wake up in the morning, what really excites me is the growth and development of our people and the collective contribution that we can make towards building the South African economy.'

## A climber's mindset

Leila believes we can only advance through intellectual growth and development, but also points out that it doesn't necessarily have to happen through academic studies. Much of her learning takes place outside the formal teaching environment.

'For example, I play chess online and that works a different part of your brain. Knowledge comes from many sources, and you need to have an open mind to learn from the most unexpected or unorthodox places. I often find life lessons in surprising places and coming from a wide range of people. Taking the time to interact with people from all walks of life helps to diversify your thought processes ... '

Another unorthodox setting where she has learnt many lessons, is on a mountain cliff. Leila has climbed Mount Elbrus, the highest peak in Russia and Europe, and she has summited Mount Vinson and Mount Kilimanjaro, the highest peaks in Antarctica and Africa, respectively.

After Leila moved to Australia, she switched to rock climbing. Her most exciting adventure was taking on a famous sea stack called The Moai on Tasmania Island, which looks like a totem pole. 'I value re-packaged knowledge and have often applied lessons from climbing to business and leadership situations,' she states. 'Climbing has helped form my outlook and leadership habits.

'Climbing is like chess in that it requires tremendous concentration to make all the right moves, which is especially important on difficult technical rock faces with fewer handholds and down climbing after a wrong move could lead to certain failure. When I climb, nothing else matters than the next hold.'

Climbing has also taught Leila the value of conviction. Dynamic moves, where handholds are out of reach, demand that the climber commits and follows through on the move. Any hesitation could make you fall.

But at the same time, a climber also has to face their vulnerabilities and be able to embrace risk and failure. During a lead climbing course, a guide taught Leila to fall. Although she found it a terrifying experience, she realised that learning to manage your discomfort breaks down barriers.

'We tend to want to feel safe and comfortable at all times. But by avoiding risk, we narrow our world to a tiny but comfortable myopia,' Leila says. 'In business, leaders who don't want to risk being challenged often surround themselves with like-minded followers. Climbing has taught me that without risk, life is dull and colourless. We need to seek out what takes us out of our comfort zone and gives us strength rather than safety.'

Leila's job takes up most of her time. But during downtime, she makes her way to Cape Town to feed her passion for climbing, which also helps relieve stress. Being outdoors gives her a sense of peace and the physical nature of climbing takes her mind off the pressures of her work, helping her to find balance.

### Learning from failure

The leadership principles Leila subscribes to today are different from the ones that were popular when she started her career. Humility, servant leadership and giving recognition to those around are what guide her. For many, these principles became more apparent during the pandemic when leaders in both business and politics had to start adhering to a new way of thinking.

'We are who we are because of those around us,' she explains. 'You can't scale the leadership totem pole if you try to do everything yourself. In the words of Isaac Newton, "If I have seen further, it is by standing on the shoulders of giants." I believe I am where I am because of the giants on whose shoulders I've stood. Leaders are a function of the people they surround themselves with and their ability to connect with, motivate and inspire them will determine their success.'

Previously it was common and accepted practice to lead by fear, dominance and aggression, but this approach does not work, Leila says. People follow leaders who display a congruent value system, which includes listening to team members. Leaders do not have to have all the right answers – but they should learn to ask the right questions if they want to gain insights from the giants around them.

True leadership is also characterised by sacrifice and the willingness to give others an opportunity to succeed. Leila cites the example of Marie Curie, who wanted to study further but instead worked and paid for her sister Bronisława to go to school. After she completed her studies, Bronisława then paid for Marie's studies and Marie eventually went on to become a two-time Nobel Prize winner.

'You can imagine the level of empathy and consideration displayed by somebody who has the mental capacity to win two Nobel prizes,' says Leila. 'These are the kinds of characteristics that create a following and motivate people to excel in a way they would never do if they were led by fear or deadlines.'

She cites another example. 'Think of Ernest Shackleton, the explorer who attempted to cross Antarctica but got trapped with his men in the ice. He led his crew to safety through unity, resourcefulness and inventiveness. Not one of the 27 men died, in a treacherous 1 200 km-long sea traverse in an open dinghy which should certainly have led to death.'

Their quest to cross the Antarctic might have failed, but as Leila points out, in leadership case studies, Shackleton is held up as an icon. She also makes a valuable point when she observes that one can learn much from failure. This is why one should not be obsessed with task-related achievements but rather look at the lessons that emerge while we are working on them.

### *Values-based leadership*

Some of the initiatives Leila has overseen at the JSE include expanding the small to medium-sized enterprise (SME) and retail market to allow the so-called man on the street to have access to capital markets, promoting financial literacy and ensuring that the pricing of trading on the market is such that people who previously could not afford to buy shares are able to do so.

According to Leila, the most important contribution she feels she has made is to help JSE staff from previously disadvantaged backgrounds grow and develop. Although she had to pay her university fees by working three different jobs, she realises there are many others who have experienced much more challenging circumstances and has deep empathy for those who have had the odds stacked against them.

Used to operating in a male-dominated industry, Leila noticed that the pandemic created a new frame for leadership and expanded the role of female leaders. 'It took us back to basic values,' she says. 'Value systems have shifted and leaders must respond to a new and evolving dynamic. People have now come to expect a more nuanced leadership style that is in touch with values.'

She points to a number of female leaders having outperformed at the highest level, including the presidents of Iceland, New Zealand and Germany. 'This new form of leadership has opened minds and created an imperative for change – the barriers to women [in leadership positions] have started to come down.'

Leila has enjoyed sponsorship and support from both male and female leaders in the past, but she believes women need to do more to assist talented young women. She says one of the most difficult barriers to development is unconscious bias. For example, people tend to hire in their likeness and so it would take a critical mass of women to achieve true equality in the workplace.

'Times are changing but much more needs to be done,' Leila observes. 'At the JSE, we have embraced female leadership – more than 50% of our board is female and more than 70% of the executive leadership is female. This stems from a conscious effort to promote female leadership. There are formal and informal mechanisms to promote the development of female leaders and it is an imperative for all female leaders to grow women around them.'

While the JSE itself is doing well on the gender scorecard, the rest of the companies listed on the bourse have yet to achieve parity when it comes to women in leadership. A PwC survey found that only 8% of the CEOs of the top 100 companies are female.

In 2021, the JSE won the World Federation of Exchanges award in the gender category for emerging market stock exchanges. According to the requirements for listing on the exchange, boards have to disclose their racial and gender composition and also share their social statistics in sustainability reporting, she says. 'What is more concerning for me is the unequal gender pay parity,' she says. 'A report by Stats SA found that South African women earn between 54% and 68% of what their male counterparts take home.'

Leila Fourie might come across as soft-spoken and restrained, but you would be wrong to judge this book by its cover. She can be fearless in business, while having the empathy to be a servant leader. With her courageous climber's mindset, who knows what she'll get up to next.

EXXARO's **Mxolisi Mgojo**
*(Photo: Courtesy of Exxaro)*

# MXOLISI MGOJO

*Innovate or die*

> 'A leader needs to be a change agent
> to get his team to think about the next big thing.
> You have two options: innovate or die.'

Exxaro CEO Mxolisi Mgojo has been pushing boundaries throughout his career.

After completing his BSc Computer Science studies at Northeastern University in Boston in the United States in 1981, Mxolisi was head-hunted by global IT solutions company Unisys to work as a programmer in the UK. Even though this has been a 'personal best achievement', the company's fortunes turned, and he was retrenched.

This gave him the time to think about where he wanted his career to go in the long term. He was in his late twenties and still had time to make dramatic changes. He decided he would do something that would teach him more than just IT, because having a narrow scope of skills had not served him well until then.

'I also wanted to experience other industries; I was eager to learn,' says Mxolisi. 'A friend set me up with an interview at Nedcor but they wanted me for an IT role, which I wasn't interested in. I wanted to learn banking. I didn't mind starting at the bottom and therefore I joined their management development programme.'

While working for Unisys in the UK, Mxolisi also developed systems for private clients on the side. He had an entrepreneurial itch that needed to be scratched. So, when an opportunity to buy a business came up in 1996, he walked away from Nedcor and joined the business with a few of his relatives. However, soon the Commonwealth Development Corporation, which was funding the business, pulled out and did a deal with the company's competitors.

'It was the second most traumatic time in my life after the Unisys retrenchment,' Mxolisi says. 'It was incredibly tough. At this moment I really saw the power of God in times of crisis. I grew up in a Christian family but you don't really get to know God until he comes into your personal space.'

Mxolisi began looking for another job in early 1997, but there were very few opportunities. After he missed several mortgage payments on his house, the bank was getting ready to repossess their family home. So when European financial services group Société Générale made him an offer to join their investment banking and corporate finance programme, he fell to his knees and gave thanks.

'Just a week later, I was offered another position at Citibank. It paid more, but I felt this second offer was God testing me. I believe He was checking whether I would be greedy, so I turned it down and stayed with Société Générale.'

### The Eyesizwe bid

Mxolisi had been with the French banking group for about a year when a friend of his invited him to lunch with entrepreneur Sipho Nkosi, who was initiating a bid to acquire the coal assets of Anglo American at the time. Together with Mandla Mchunu, Nkosi had put together a consortium of black businessmen under the Eyesizwe umbrella. Fifteen minutes into the meal, he invited Mxolisi to become part of his team.

Mxolisi told him he knew nothing about mining and said he doubted he would be of any value. But Nkosi was charming and a real gentleman, the kind of guy people wanted to know and have a professional relationship with. So, when he called Mxolisi three weeks later and asked him to pass by his office, Mxolisi obliged.

Again Nkosi asked him to join their team, and again Mxolisi declined.

Precious minerals such as diamonds and gold would have been an attractive prospect, but coal could make Mxolisi think only of the dirty and dusty parts of northern South Africa.

A month later the ever persistent Nkosi invited Mxolisi to meet him at a hotel. This time they were joined by Chris Morris from PwC's corporate finance division. Before Mxolisi could say anything, Nkosi asked him to explain what he does at Société Générale.

'I have a portfolio of clients for whom I provide debt refinancing, structured finance and similar services,' Mxolisi said.

'So, you work with a team of international experts, you analyse companies and try find opportunities through financial engineering, which would then add value to them?' Nkosi asked.

Mxolisi nodded in agreement.

'Between ideation and execution, what is the hardest of the two?' Nkosi pressed on.

'Securing the mandate is 70% of the work,' Mxolisi replied. 'Because once that is done, the execution is quite easy.'

'So, you mean to tell me that you can put together such difficult finance proposals for big companies, but you would struggle to sell a black piece of rock?' Nkosi asked.

A stunned Mxolisi was left without words. The task Nkosi had in mind for him did indeed sound straightforward – he would become the marketing and logistics manager of their start-up, which would soon be called Eyesizwe Coal. The die was cast. Yet it was quite a daunting prospect to market a start-up. What's more, the team didn't yet include any mining people, and everyone thought of them as rank outsiders.

'We were the donkeys that dared to show up at the Durban July,' Mxolisi recalls with a smile. 'I think what won it for us is that we decided to put skin in the game. We put up a lot of our own money to demonstrate our commitment, because the business could not handle high gearing. We advised PwC that we didn't have the money to pay their rates and instead offered them 4% equity.'

They decided that for their final bidding document they needed a vision for their company and to be purposeful in what they were trying to create. They stated that they would use the asset to create the building blocks for a diverse resources and energy business that would be rooted in South Africa but have a global footprint. In 2001, Eyesizwe Coal outbid 64 other companies in the acquisition of the coal assets of Anglo American and Billiton.

### Expanding Exxaro

Eyesizwe Coal achieved great success and had proven itself as a serious player by 2006, when it merged with Kumba Resources' non-iron ore assets to form Exxaro. 'The transaction was hailed as the deal of the year, singled out for being head and shoulders above the rest in terms of black management participation, the level of economic interest held by black people, as well as the extent of voting rights held by black people,' *Forbes Africa* reported.

Since then, Exxaro has grown to become one of the biggest black-empowered and most diversified mining companies in South Africa. The company operates facilities and offices in Africa, Asia, Europe and Australia. It is listed on the Johannesburg Stock Exchange and on 31 December 2021 had assets of R75.7 billion and a market capitalisation of R53.4 billion.

But helping to establish the company was not always smooth sailing for Mxolisi. As a newcomer to mining, he had to learn everything from scratch and he had to put together a marketing department without the required qualifications.

'I first needed to learn the business of coal because you can't market something that you don't understand. I had to build a marketing and logistics business over five years and sell coal to both domestic and international customers. In banking I was just a professional, but in Eyesizwe, I quickly had to learn to manage a division of 4 000 people with businesses in Inner Mongolia, Namibia and South Africa.'

After a restructuring process in 2008, Mxolisi ended up heading the biggest division – coal. He had been tracking the renewable energy sector and told Nkosi that a time was coming when it would also have an impact on South Africa. In 2009, they decided to form a renewable energy division in Exxaro. Their perspective on coal had changed – they now saw it as an energy resource rather than as a mining resource.

'It's an alternative fuel and therefore we could conceptualise other forms of energy, such as gas and biothermal. In 2012, we started a project that was housed under a company called Cennergi, which participates in the government's Renewable Energy Independent Power Producers Programme. Cennergi has projects that generate over 200 megawatts of power. Who would think that a fossil fuel company would invest in renewables?'

In 2014, Mxolisi had an opportunity to be in the running for the CEO position. He had to present a ten-year strategy. Part of his plan was to look at how technology could become a game changer in their business, and he tried to understand how big companies that had been really successful at some point, such as Nokia, Kodak and Blockbuster, somehow ended up in the corporate graveyard.

'So I went to Singularity University in San Francisco for their executive leadership programme, which gave me insight into what was happening in Silicon Valley. It helped me understand technology and how I could redefine my strategy. Trimming our head office by half, I realised, would bring down our costs significantly.'

### Becoming a tech-driven CEO

Mxolisi crafted a winning strategy and in May 2015 he was announced the CEO designate. A year later when he took over from Nkosi, he enlisted in a programme at Futureworld, an organisation that helps leaders design businesses that will be disruptive in the future. They allowed him to bring in members of his team and Mxolisi roped in his executive committee, middle managers and the millennials at Exxaro. Soon they were talking about robotics and the internet of things – a system of connected machines and computers that talk to each other over a network, without needing human input.

Mxolisi came up with the idea to build a fully digitally operated mine. People thought he was crazy. But in November 2017, Exxaro started to build a first-of-its-kind digital mine at Belfast in Mpumalanga and it was ready for operation by February 2020, completed ahead of schedule and within budget.

It was a great challenge to get the whole organisation to start thinking about a future in a way that it has never been thought about. Mxolisi had to get his executives to understand and appreciate what was possible.

'I also spent time learning and understanding companies like Ørsted, who transitioned from fossil fuels to renewable energy,' Mxolisi explains.

'I'm not a Formula One racing fan, but I looked at how McLaren managed to transform their team. All other car makers had fast cars and great drivers, but what was it about McLaren that made them so successful?

'What happens in the pit stop is what wins races. You can be the best driver on the course, but if you spend more time having your tyres changed during the pit stop than your competitor, you have no chance of winning.'

In the book *A Beautiful Constraint: How to Transform Your Limitations into Advantages, and Why It's Everyone's Business*, Adam Morgan and Mark Barden explain how McLaren installed cameras to record each of the 20 people in the pit crew. Using technology, they worked on improving personal times, which helped them cut pit-stop time from 4 seconds to a world record of 2.5 seconds. The team now believes it is not money but efficiency that drives performance. The practice of micro-analysis and continual improvement has become part of McLaren's culture.

Mxolisi asked himself what Exxaro's pit stop was and how they could improve efficiency. So the company investigated how it could use technology to this end and sent teams to the Accenture Technology Hub in Ireland and the German energy company RWE to look at lean applications. From those experiences, each function had to apply new thinking and innovation and Exxaro created a unit charged with driving business excellence and transformation.

'We brought in things like robotics to handle repetitive and boring tasks. At Exxaro, robots are doing a lot of work at odd hours. We also required our service providers, such as our internal auditors, to innovate. We made it clear that they needed to adopt a digital view if they wanted to service us in the future. They started their own process of reinvention, and so we are also helping our suppliers become competitive.'

### *Powering possibilities*

Mxolisi also asked employees which part of their jobs they didn't enjoy. Accountants, for example, complained that month-end reporting took too long, so he challenged them to adopt technology to cut the 14-day process by half. If you automate a bad process, you only make an inappropriate thing work faster, he says, so the team needed to design their own processes. It was an exciting exercise, because they could let technology do the things they didn't like and they ended up with higher-quality work and doing the more meaningful tasks that were part of their job description.

'I had to bring in the unions and spend days showing them how workforces had been impacted by this process in other companies. I helped them understand what we were trying to achieve to allay fears that jobs would be lost and explained that we would rather be reskilling our labour force. The HR [human resources] department had to come up with a whole new learning platform to make our workforce relevant for future jobs.'

For Mxolisi, leadership is about how you inspire people. When he sent out teams to learn from innovative companies internationally, they got exposed to best practice and came back rearing to go. 'They were so pumped. I couldn't hold them back!' he remembers.

'Our payoff line is "Powering possibilities" – we can power what seems impossible to make it possible. It is all about playing in the change-agent space, which is something that I have always been comfortable doing. You cannot be complacent; you need to think ahead. For example, at our [digital] Belfast mine the average age of our workers is just under 35 years, but in a conventional mine it is much higher because people generally need at least 20 years of experience.'

According to Mxolisi, the digital age means a workforce doesn't need as many years of experience because so much of the work that has traditionally required experience can be done using analytics and artificial intelligence. 'Experience is not going to save you. A guy at Kodak invented the digital camera and they ignored him because they were the biggest photography company and thought they knew it all. The lesson is to always be on the lookout for new things.'

'My philosophy is to get out of the village. If you grow up in a village and never leave, you will believe the only way of life is that of the village. That is until you visit the next village, then the nearest town and later advanced cities. The same applies to companies that create a village mentality around their success, believing that things will always remain constant. But they never do. A leader needs to be a change agent to get his team to think about what the next big thing is. You have two options: innovate or die.'

At a glittering ceremony held at Sun City in June 2022, Mxolisi was named Business Leader of the Year at the All Africa Business Leaders Award.

His advice to future business leaders? 'Think big, have a daring vision and seek mentors who can guide and encourage you through the many difficult patches on your road to success,' he answers.

A new era awaited the change agent at Exxaro after his retirement in July last year. He told me he would be taking a sabbatical and also looks forward to spending more time with his grandkids.

'And I'm going to get into mountain biking – I'm currently training for an eight-day race. I am also part of Business Leadership South Africa, through which we will be supporting the government to deal with the issues our country is facing. I'm not keen to sit on corporate boards; I'd much rather look at how I can assist in socioeconomic issues,' he concludes.

**PwC AFRICA's Dion Shango**
*(Photo: Courtesy of PwC)*

# DION SHANGO

*The paradigm of 'authentegrity'*

'Trust is an incredibly precious and fragile thing.
It takes decades to earn, but you can destroy it in an instant.'

I first met Dion Shango at his then Sunninghill office in Johannesburg in 2016, less than a year after he became CEO of PwC Southern Africa. His appointment was quite an accomplishment for a 39-year-old and his excitement was still evident – he grinned from ear to ear throughout our one-hour interview for the SA Professional Services Awards. Despite not winning the Accounting Professional of the Year Award for which he was a finalist, he leapt up to congratulate Ebrahim Dhorat of EY, that year's winner, and later expressed how delighted he had been just to be nominated.

When we meet again, it is six years later. Yet Dion is as amicable as before, even if there is slightly more of a seriousness around him this time. I wonder if it is due to his being Africa CEO, responsible for the entire PwC business across the continent, since July 2019. Has he been hardened by the challenges of leading an international consulting firm in tumultuous times? Or perhaps it simply has to do with getting older and realising how lonely it is at the top?

I ask Dion how he remains authentic while fulfilling his CEO role, which requires him to grow the fee base of the company (PwC is the largest audit firm by fees in South Africa.)

'When I took over as Africa CEO, I could easily have decided that I'm no longer involved in client delivery,' he says. 'Instead, I took the decision to retain some of the clients where I'm the lead engagement partner. For territory CEOs to be involved in client delivery is something that is extremely rare and unusual in the PwC network, but I felt it was a way of really demonstrating to the partners that I'm in the trenches with them. Our strategy is underpinned by high quality standards and what better way to demonstrate commitment to that strategy than to get involved in its first-hand execution?'

### Truthfully principled

His many years in leadership – he was appointed as a partner at 32 – have taught Dion the power of working as part of a team. However, he recognises that not even the leadership team will always have all the answers to the problems the company faces and that they need to consult widely to find lasting solutions.

In her book *Extraordinary Leadership*, trainer and consultant Cher Holton introduces the concept of 'authentegrity'. The portmanteau combines two essential qualities of a good leader: authenticity and integrity. Holton writes that people want to be led by someone 'real' and that leadership therefore demands the expression of an authentic self.

'Try to lead like someone else, and you will fail. Employees will not follow leaders who invest little of themselves in their leadership behaviours. This is partly a reaction to the turbulent times we live in. Our growing dissatisfaction with sleek, artificial, airbrushed leadership is what makes Authentegrity such a desirable quality in today's business world – a quality that, unfortunately, is in short supply. Leaders and followers both associate Authentegrity with sincerity, honesty, and integrity.'

Holton argues that one can achieve authentegrity by analysing what one's signature strengths are and applying them to one's everyday life. Authentic leaders are constantly learning from their leadership experiences. They respond to their intrinsic motives rather than being influenced by power, money, recognition or expediency. Their thoughts and actions originate from within them; they are secure in their integrity to resist destructive external pressures.

Following a number of corporate failures, which many argue could have been averted if high auditing standards were upheld, many consulting firms in South Africa, in my opinion, are facing a crisis of authentegrity. PwC has not been spared public scrutiny in its engagements, with two particular assignments from the recent past making the news.

As auditors of South African Airways (SAA), PwC was criticised for their conduct by the Zondo Commission [of Inquiry into Allegations of State Capture]. The firm has taken full responsibility, admitting that they fell short of the high standards expected of them. Dion explains that they have taken the necessary remedial action by improving audit methodology, specifically in relation to public sector audits. They have also strengthened certain aspects of risk management internally in relation to client acceptance and continuance.

The second matter relates to a consulting engagement at the national power utility in 2016. In June 2020, Eskom issued a letter of demand to the firm for R95 million as a refund of fees. The basis of the claim was that in Eskom's assessment, the manner in which the work was procured was irregular and that PwC was allegedly paid for work done by Eskom's own employees. PwC disagreed with claims after internal investigations at the firm found no basis on which to entertain Eskom's demand. More than two years later, Eskom has yet to take legal action, despite threatening to do so.

Dion has learnt to be brave and stay true to both his personal and corporate values. 'In the heat of the moment, it is not always easy to call things for what they are. Take for example the SAA situation: had we applied ourselves to risk management considerations in continuing that audit, things would have been different. We need to be transparent and robust in the assessment of risk.'

Dion says leading PwC has revealed to him how 'incredibly precious and valuable' a brand can be. 'Our new focus is on building trust and delivering sustained outcomes. Trust is an incredibly important and fragile thing. It takes decades to earn, but you can destroy it in an instant. PwC as a brand is representative of trust and it is important for all of us to remember that. The brand has been built over 160 years and we have been entrusted for a limited time to look after it and ensure that we bequeath it to the next generation in a better and more trusted position than we found it.'

Corporate values were the focus of PwC's recent employee survey. It asked the 250 000 employees worldwide which values they would like to see embodied by the organisation they work for. 'The responses distilled to integrity, care, working together, re-imagining the possible and making a difference,' Dion says.

### Retaining partners and people

PwC has three main business lines, including risk assurance, which is the bedrock of the company. The taxation division is also a steady income earner. The third offering is advisory, which comprises corporate finance, forensic investigations, mergers and acquisitions, and dispute resolution.

'Advisory is trickier in the sense that you compete with multiple organisations, even those that are dissimilar to you,' Dion explains. 'Our challenge has been finding our niche and making a success of it at the right price point. I have been working with the leader of that business to try and stabilise it and make certain that partners in the business remain engaged.'

In recent times Dion also faced a challenge in relation to the South African business when the implementation of a new system did not go according to plan. This had a negative impact on the partners, which meant they had to restore their belief in PwC and its future again. To achieve that they had to find new ways of communicating with their partners, which Dion pioneered by creating a weekly newsletter.

'This has never been done before,' he states. 'It ensured that we stay connected to our partners and they were kept up to date about the journey we were on to restore stability in our business. This continues today, with Shirley Machaba [the new PwC Southern Africa CEO] writing one every two weeks and me doing it monthly for our Africa practice.'

According to Dion running a professional services firm is different from running other types of businesses such as manufacturing, retail or mining, because it is people orientated. The company culture is critical and employees want to be fulfilled in their work. They also want to feel valued, which underscores the importance of one of PwC's values – that of care. 'It is important for firms to keep their employees engaged, while attracting and retaining the best talent,' says Dion.

When the PwC leadership formulated their strategy, it was clear to Dion that it had to be for the long term, rather than one that would serve them only during their stint as the leadership team.

It also had to be clear, simple, coherent and easy to remember. 'A strategy shouldn't be a document of many pages, but rather a whole picture on a single page. People should be able to understand the page, engage with its message and resonate with the objective. The proof of a good strategy lies in its execution and it can only be successfully executed if it's easily understood.'

A strategy guides an organisation's decision-making, and Dion believes it is impossible to be an effective leader if you're not decisive.

'I would rather make the wrong decision than none at all. Procrastination is never the answer. Decision-making is difficult because of the impact it has on people's lives. For example, at the beginning of the [COVID-19] pandemic we decided that we would not retrench our staff even though we knew there would be a negative financial impact on our bottom line. We were able to stick to that decision for two years.'

While the company had to restructure and lay off staff since then, Dion explains that this was already on the cards before the pandemic. He describes this restructuring and the fact that he could not travel and engage with other teams across the continent as the low points of his term so far as Africa CEO.

### *The importance of soft skills*

Dion did not plan on taking up the top seat of one of Africa's largest consulting firms as a young finance professional. By his own admission, he is quite shy and he gets extremely nervous when he has to address large groups. This surprises many people as he comes across as a natural at public speaking.

'Becoming a partner was already a significant milestone in my career,' he says. 'The additional layer of leadership that comes with my current position is interesting because as CEO of a partnership you are a CEO of other CEOs; each partner essentially has his own business comprising a portfolio of clients and a team of managers. To become a CEO, one needs to recognise that many people have the technical skills, but it is the emotional intelligence that distinguishes leaders from followers.'

He points out that being able to show empathy and to interact with others appropriately are what set good leaders apart. These skills are difficult to teach and replicate. His advice to future CEOs is to always think about how they can develop their soft skills – which is much harder than advancing technical skills. Attributes such as effective communication, being a team player, engaging new clients and managing difficult ones are learnt over time.

'Furthermore, the digital era has redefined how we engage as human beings. This means there is the additional challenge of remaining an effective leader at a time when human connections are not what they used to be. Leadership is about knowing what's important to your people, understanding what inspires them and knowing which buttons to press.'

Dion views success as something that is about more than just oneself. 'It goes beyond financial prosperity; it's about effecting growth in people,' he says. He was very excited, for example, that the appointment of new partners in July 2022 raised the percentage of partners from previously disadvantaged communities to 40% in South Africa.

'Across the continent, we have also increased our diversity by raising

242

our proportion of female partners to 28%. We might not get everything right yet, but that is fine – our failures beget success. It is only by learning from our mistakes that we will build authenticity and character,' he concludes.

WEBBER WENTZEL's **Sally Hutton**
*(Photo: Zaid Joseph)*

# SALLY HUTTON

## The advocate for multi-pronged solutions

'I believe complex problems require multi-pronged solutions.
You cannot just do one or two things – you must develop a plan
that addresses the problem from multiple angles ... '

As managing partner at Webber Wentzel, Sally Hutton is known for her expert legal work, but what many people don't know is that to friends and family she is also known as a poodle ambassador. She is completely enchanted by this breed of dogs and has three that she routinely spoils rotten. One of them was a gift from a friend for her fiftieth birthday during the hard lockdown in May 2020 – the friend took advantage of a loophole in the regulations that listed livestock as an essential product!

Sally loves the law almost as much as she loves poodles. She has always been fascinated by how laws are developed and refined and believes she is a good match for the field considering her proficiency in language, as well as her problem-solving and analytical skills.

Born in 1970, Sally and her sister grew up in Cape Town to a father who was a chemical engineer and mother who was a qualified physiotherapist. In 1992, she graduated top of her BA (LLB) class at the University of Cape Town and was awarded the Patrick and Margaret Flanagan Scholarship to study at Oxford University in the UK. During her interview for the scholarship, she made it clear that she intended to return to South Africa after her studies to contribute to the country, using the knowledge and experience she had acquired. She graduated with a Master of Studies in Law degree from Oxford in 1994 and joined Webber Wentzel as a candidate attorney the following year.

'Throughout my childhood, my parents emphasised the mantra "dare to be different", which I think was really great for two young girls growing up in the 1970s and 1980s,' she reminisces. 'It gave us the confidence and conviction that we could become whatever we wanted to, without any gender constraints. At home, there was also a general commitment to hard work and excellence, which I think drove me throughout my studies and career.

'Shortly after commencing my articles, I did a second master's degree in Taxation Law at Wits [University of the Witwatersrand]. My dissertation was on the taxation of derivatives, which aligned with my initial practice focus area of derivatives law. Later I moved into the area of private equity mergers and acquisitions, which I loved and still practise today.'

### On balancing a career and motherhood

Sally's three children were born at different stages of her career, and she worked part time for about seven years. She was a second-year associate when she had her first baby, a junior salaried partner by the time the second was born, and an equity partner when the third came along.

'In some ways, it is easier when you are in a junior role because you are part of a team and you're not facing clients. Senior colleagues take ultimate responsibility and since you have not yet established yourself, it's less disruptive to your practice. Later in your career, when you are in a senior role, you have more flexibility as a partner but you also have a greater degree of accountability, which can present a challenge when trying to balance work and personal commitments.'

What was key to Sally's ability to navigate this period was that she had a mentor and champion in Webber Wentzel's previous senior partner, David Lancaster. She worked in his practice and when she fell pregnant with her first child, she was asked to write the firm's first maternity policy. At the time, she thought the policy was quite reasonable even though it is much more generous today.

The hallmark of her career at the firm and as a mother was the support she received. 'I don't think anyone should have to choose between having a career and being a parent. It is possible to have both a rewarding career and a rewarding family life, but you can't do it alone. It requires support, teamwork and flexibility from those at work and at home. You need to acknowledge that you can't do it all on your own and you must ask for help.

'Recently, I read something very pertinent: "You cannot measure your career using somebody else's ruler." Do not try to align yourself to others; do what is right for you, based on your own timing, and do it at your own pace.'

After Sally had her third child, she felt it was time to step up the pace and she started showing an interest in the leadership of the firm. By 2010, for example, she was leading her own practice group, had been elected to the firm's management board and was a member of various committees, including those looking at equity partner remuneration and talent management at the firm. She also chaired the firm's transformation committee.

Serving in these positions allowed her to gain experience in strategy development and execution. In 2012, she attended a course at Harvard Business School on leading professional services firms, which gave her invaluable insights into the unique challenges of law firm leadership.

### Managing partner

In 2014, Webber Wentzel's then senior partner unexpectedly fell ill and announced that he would be stepping down. Sally's partners encouraged her to stand for election. Given how the firm had grown in size and complexity, management decided to split the position of senior partner into two. Christo Els was elected Senior Partner and Sally Managing Partner, effective 1 March 2015. Since then, she has had to balance her leadership responsibilities with her practice as a private equity lawyer.

There are about 130 equity partners at Webber Wentzel – all highly intelligent, highly educated and independently minded. They are also very invested, because each of them is an owner of the business. The structure of the CEO's role here is therefore different from that at a listed company, which is more hierarchical, says Sally. Another defining feature is that leaders are peer elected and not appointed.

'For me that means that our roles are about service leadership,' she says. 'My leadership role is centred on persuading people to take actions that are in the best interest of the firm. Issuing instructions does not work!

'Leading other lawyers can be challenging, because people have many different points of view. But in that there's also the opportunity to harness that diversity of thought. We have to ensure the firm runs smoothly but also allow enough time for debate and consultation. As the leadership of the firm, we always strive to achieve a broad consensus on the way forward.'

Sally chairs the executive committee and Christo the board. While both structures are responsible for strategy formulation, the board is responsible for partnership type issues, stakeholder management and risk management, while the Exco sees to execution of the strategy and the day-to-day running of the firm. The board and Exco work closely together and are supported by a highly skilled professional business services team led by the firm's chief operating officer. That team includes the chief financial officer, chief information officer and human resources director, among others. The firm recently also appointed a director of client and culture because they believe these are the key areas in which they can differentiate themselves from other similar law firms.

### *Weathering storms with strong leadership and strategy*

When I ask Sally about the attributes of a good strategy, she repeats what I have heard many other CEOs say: a strategy must be clear, simple and executable. It should provide a vision of the future and a plan for how to get there. Vague strategies are difficult to distil into concrete actions.

Furthermore, a good strategy should have an underlying purpose that helps to bond your organisation. When Webber Wentzel last refined their strategy, they formally articulated their purpose, which is 'to have a transformative and sustainable impact through our work and actions'. This is not only linked to the positive impact they seek to have through client work but also reflects their collective social conscience through, for example, pro bono work.

Sally points out that a strategy should also be flexible. Once you set yourself on a path, you must be able to tweak your strategy should circumstances or the market change. Every year, the firm reconsiders its strategy and the targets it has set and makes the necessary adjustments. It is also crucial for a strategy to be properly measured and tracked to ensure that you are constantly moving forward. Webber Wentzel believes in setting ambitious goals as a way to keep people inspired, motivated and moving in the same direction.

When a strategy is properly aligned with a firm's different structures and processes, everyone knows where they fit in, says Sally.

In the initial stages of the pandemic, when deals were being cancelled and mandates terminated, there was much anxiety at law firms, particularly around liquidity. In South African law firms, the individual partners are all liable for the debts of the firm. That period of uncertainty called for strong leadership, says Sally.

'I believe complex problems require multi-pronged solutions. You can't do just one or two things – you must develop a plan that addresses the problem from several angles. We very quickly formulated a COVID-19 response plan by applying first principles and ultimately relying on common sense. The plan put our people and our clients first and tackled the issues with a range of initiatives not only to support our clients quickly but also to drive liquidity management, people management and culture. This included enhanced transparency and connectedness, and improved morale.'

From a leadership perspective, the pandemic represented a career high for Sally because it was so gratifying to see their response plan work and staff come together and collaborate to weather the storm successfully. Another high is the unprecedented growth in revenue and profitability since 2015. They have also won several awards, including the Empowering Women in the Workplace Award at the 2021 Accenture Gender Mainstreaming Awards.

### *Making great strides for gender equality*

Sally herself has received two accolades from the SA Professional Services Awards – Woman Professional of the Year in 2016 and Overall Professional of the Year in 2018. She was the first South African woman to be mentioned in the coveted Chambers' Band 1 (their highest ranking) for private equity mergers and acquisitions work. She was recently shortlisted as one of five finalists for the RMB Africa's Fearless Thinker Award, in recognition of her thought leadership in tackling gender mainstreaming issues.

'It has been very rewarding experiencing the increasing depth and diversity of our talent. From a personal perspective, one of my proudest moments was in March 2022 when, after our most recent round of partner promotions, women made up 49% of our partners. When I first initiated our formal gender strategy in 2015, we set a target of achieving a 50-50 gender mix in our partnership by 2022. That was a very audacious goal at the time, since women made up only 35% of our partnership then.'

Sally says she is grateful that she has not experienced much overt discrimination in her career. Still, there were a few instances where she encountered gender bias. For example, once when she went with a junior colleague to a client, the client assumed that he was in charge simply because he was a man.

In 2015, Sally became the first female managing partner of a big corporate law firm in South Africa. With many other women since having been appointed in senior leadership roles in big law firms in the country, one can say she paved the way.

I ask her whether she feels she may have missed out on other opportunities, given that she's been with the same firm throughout her career. She's had many approaches over the years, all of which she has turned down, she answers.

'It would have been easy to leave if I wasn't constantly challenged and stimulated by my career at the firm. I feel that I've been constantly growing – in the more than 27 years I've been here, both the firm and my role have changed significantly. It gave me with unbelievable learning opportunities. There have been many interesting transactions and I have worked with amazing clients, colleagues and opposing counsel from other firms. I have done transactions in multiple sectors and therefore learnt a lot about different industries and business models.'

## *Intrinsically motivated to lead*

As the leader of a law firm, you need to earn the respect and trust of your peers, Sally says. You should be known as someone who is fair, honest and principled and that you always put the interests of the firm first. Importantly, you should also have a vision and know how to bridge the gap between the present and the future. Good leaders are curious and open to learn. Transparency is also key to building trust.

'A leader must be able to take ideas from multiple sources,' Sally advises. 'I think the strength of our leadership team comes from the ability to collaborate across disciplines. It has been proven that diverse leadership teams produce better decision-making and results, and that has certainly been our firm's experience.

'You must also be a good communicator and have the ability to think strategically, while keeping an eye on the detail and being strong on execution. COVID-19 proved that good leaders know how to flex their thinking and adapt.'

Future leaders learn a lot through experience – doing things a certain way and then realising that they could have done them differently. Fully formed leaders do not emerge at birth; leadership skills are learnt through trial and error, Sally says. Those who are open to doing things differently and applying learnings from success in one area to another are most likely to succeed in a rapidly changing environment where innovation is key.

'What do you think leads to success in a leadership role?' I ask.

'It boils down to what motivates you to take on the role,' Sally responds. 'The reason I wanted this job was that I care deeply about Webber Wentzel and its future.' It was never about the title or status, she says. She believes the best leaders are those who are intrinsically, rather than externally, motivated to lead. They want to make an impact and improve the organisation for the generation that will follow them.

After chatting to Sally for an hour, I see why she has a strong preference for a particular German dog breed. People who own poodles say these dogs are intelligent, alert, active, faithful and willing to learn; adjectives that can also be used to describe the human being who has been called their ambassador.

# PETER STEENKAMP

*Leadership with a sense of humour*

'Trust is something that is earned. Leaders must be dependable
and have a reputation for doing the right thing –
and show this in everything they do.'

In 1977, Peter Steenkamp enrolled for a degree in quantity surveying at the University of Pretoria, but soon realised it was not his cup of tea. Fortunately, his roommate at residence suggested he work at a mine during the holidays to pass the time. Peter fell in love with the work, because he was not confined to an office desk, could spend hours with 'real people' underground and could emerge into the glaring sun with shiny finds each day.

There and then he applied for a scholarship to do mining engineering and changed his course elective at varsity. He graduated in the summer of 1982 and became the first person in his family to go into mining, a career he says fit his personality like a glove. His formal career started at Gold Fields, where he worked as a shift boss, followed by joining Vaal Reefs, an Anglo American Gold operation, in 1989. At Vaal Reefs, he held various positions, steadily rising to the position of business unit manager by 1997.

'I was a youngster in my thirties charged with running what was a pretty big mine,' Peter recalls. 'This experience developed my leadership skills since I had to manage over 4 000 people. We were putting together a mine operation, which meant that my organisational skills were also put to the test. Seeing a mine develop from inception to a

AFRICA RAINBOW MINERALS, PAMODZI GOLD
& HARMONY GOLD's **Peter Steenkamp**
*(Photo: Justin Barlow, Eimage)*

functioning entity producing viable resources was incredibly satis-fying.'

The early stages of his career exposed Peter to the use of technology in mining. At Vaal Reef's Number 10 shaft, he saw for the first time how seismic surveys to explore underground mineral resources were being used. In addition, the operation produced high volumes using hydro power and employing double blasting.

In 1998, Peter joined Patrice Motsepe's ARMgold as a business unit leader and later became one of the directors of operations. He was involved in running the joint venture Free Gold and also took part in the listing of ARMgold on the Johannesburg Stock Exchange in 2002. Of the many initiatives undertaken at ARMgold, Peter is especially proud of implementing continuous operations.

'We operated the mine for 24 hours a day, seven days a week,' he explains. 'Together with the relevant labour unions, we formulated a work programme for our employees that involved two seven-day cycles with one off-day in between, then a seven-day shift with five days' rest. Workers signed employee contracts to that effect, so we managed to run it successfully and had profitable mines up until they came to the end of their economic life.'

Peter is a great fan of continuous operations, even if it's not easy to implement in South Africa because of the country's strict labour laws and getting ministerial approval for work on Sundays. He has even de-veloped a case study that demonstrates how continuous operations can boost production without a commensurate increase in costs.

In 2003, ARMgold merged with Harmony Gold. A restructure of the operations of the two entities resulted in all gold mining entities being moved to Harmony, with Africa Rainbow Minerals (ARM) housing the rest of the resources. As a result, Peter was appointed chief operating officer at Harmony Gold.

Four years later, he took up the role of CEO of Pamodzi Gold. But this turned out to be a low point in Peter's career. The company's strat-egy was to grow annual production to a million ounces within a few years. 'Pamodzi's strategy experienced headwinds as a result of the global financial crisis in 2008. We simply could not get the finance to deliver on our plans. We needed to recapitalise the mines that had been acquired from the company but did not get the funding in time. Being an entity owned by BEE [black economic empowerment] shareholders, it was also not possible to dilute the investors through other parties that lacked these credentials. Eventually we had to go into business rescue and ultimately liquidation.'

Peter resigned in 2009, but the worst was that many people he had brought into the company from his previous stations lost their jobs. They were not only his colleagues, but also his friends.

After Pamodzi Peter joined the petrochemical group Sasol, where he held various positions, the last one being senior vice president of mining. He returned to Harmony Gold in 2016, taking over as CEO from Graham Briggs.

### Peter's nine leadership commandments

Over the years, Peter has developed nine commandments that he believes a good leader should follow to achieve success. He shares them with me one by one.

*1. Thou shalt create a vision.* 'A leader must be a master at selecting the right strategy and be able to create a compelling argument about its logic to get buy-in from all stakeholders,' he says.

Peter is a big rugby fan and he believes there are many comparisons to be drawn between the sport and leadership. For example, no matter what the game plan is before the match, 'you have to play what is in front of you'. With that he means that you need to think through situations as they arise and take advantage of opportunities.

When Peter joined ARMgold, the company made a loss and they had to come up with a strategy that would turn around the company. A similar situation prevailed when he joined Harmony: the company had a lot of debt and was looking to grow its market capitalisation. In both cases, management had to ask themselves which assets they required to reach their goals.

'After identifying the right assets, we had to craft a convincing narrative with the appropriate justification for our stakeholders to support us in our quest. At Harmony, we also needed to negotiate a sensible package for the sellers, AngloGold Ashanti, to convince them it was a suitable exit for them. That's the difficult part of executing your vision: you must be able to communicate it to those who matter and bring them on board to make it happen.'

*2. Thou shalt be trustworthy.* Leaders must be dependable and have a reputation for doing the right thing – and show this in everything they do, he says.

'You need to stick to your principles and, again, as in rugby, play the ball and not the man,' Peter professes. 'Trust is something that is earned. You cannot gain trust if you do not spend time with people. This is something I learnt from my mentor, Andre Wilkens [former CEO of ARM]. He demonstrated the importance of being approachable – having an office with open doors and no restricted areas where executives are out of reach.

'Everyone in the business should be able to have an audience with you and this includes people who are not necessarily in your purview. Members of staff who are at the lowest levels and union leaders who you frequently butt heads with should feel that they can come to you and talk about their issues.

'I grew up in apartheid South Africa, where middle management was made up solely of white men. Today these spaces are beginning to reflect the demographics of the country. I consciously try to build relationships with people from different backgrounds, also beyond the workplace. Good leaders should try to understand what is going on in the personal lives of their charges.'

*3. Thou shalt create a sense of belonging.* South Africans are generally proud of their country and happy to fly the flag, Peter observes. He believes the Springboks would never win a World Cup if the players did not love their country. Unfortunately, in the corporate arena, many workers are not proud of the companies they work for and do not have a sense of loyalty.

'It is part of a leader's job to create a tangible feeling in employees that they're part of a winning team. They need to be mentored to believe in themselves and to believe in the company. This is the only way to encourage them to promote the brand and to celebrate the company's achievements. You should be concerned when employees appear not to want to be at work.'

4. *Surround thyself with champions.* Peter says good leaders should have the ability to spot champions. 'You are not going to win a rugby game if you do not have a winger who can run 100 metres in ten seconds. A leader should constantly be on the lookout for that Bryan Habana and must mentor candidates to deliver. Inevitably, this means that some people will have to be removed from their roles and others will never progress to senior roles. Leaders should not be afraid to part ways with those who are bringing the team down.'

5. *Thou shalt be a good listener.* 'It's quite easy to let ego get in the way of managing people,' Peter warns. 'Because of the high title you hold, you get sucked into a zone where you end up believing your opinions are the most valuable. There can never be true engagement with staff if you cut people off when they are trying to express their views. This can be catastrophic in environments such as ours where union leaders want to know they've been heard. If they feel their views have been ignored, it could result in months of standoffs that disrupt the business significantly.'

6. *Thou shalt build genuine relationships.* Peter says this goes for relationships both within the organisation and with external stakeholders. Just like trust, respect is earned. Stakeholder management involves a broad group of people, including government and community leaders, who are not directly invested in company affairs.

Peter is very aware that building solid relationships with others involve an investment of time, which can be difficult when you find yourself in a high-powered role with ambitious targets and tight deliverables. Still, he says, a leader must understand that interpersonal skills are as vital, if not more important, than technical skills.

Having solid relationships has often helped Peter in his career, especially when it comes to wage negotiations with workers on mines. In 1987, during the costliest mineworker strike in South African history, Peter was responsible for the Venterspost Gold Mine, which he managed to keep open because of the relationships he had with the workers.

'If you have a connection with workers' leaders, you can always find a way forward. When there is a problem, go and meet with the worker representatives personally and hear them out; do not make the mistake of sending someone to sort things out on your behalf,' he advises.

*7. Thou shalt focus on quality and excellence.* Good leaders should set the example by not setting the bar merely at 'good enough' but at 'excellent'. You should create a company culture where high standards are upheld and quality is valued, Peter believes.

*8. Thou shalt have a sense of humour.* This is the eighth lesson in Peter's book. 'I'm a firm believer in having fun, something I share with my mentor Andre Wilkens. One time we had a very tense board meeting and a non-executive director demanded to know what we would do if management didn't do what was required of them. Wilkens calmly replied: "Ma'am, we shall break their fingers!" Everybody laughed and from that point on the discussion was relaxed.'

*9. Thou shalt not lose sight of business principles.* A leader cannot run a company without the right business acumen. You have to understand the balance sheet yourself and not leave it to the chief financial officer to balance the books, Peter says. Good CEOs also have cost discipline; they don't come up with exciting ideas without considering how the capital will be sourced and the ensuing expenses will be met. The focus must always be on the fundamentals that will make the business viable and ensure growth.

### Beyond work

Peter's counsel extends beyond business to life in general. He is set to complete a pastoral narrative therapy course that is giving him the tools to help people with problems such as depression, divorce and anxiety. 'I decided to do the course during the COVID-19 lockdown. I found it very difficult to cope with sitting idle and not being productive. I realised this would be my life in a couple of years' time and that was when I made the call to start investing in how I can give back when the curtain falls on my executive career.'

Peter believes that success is also about finding inner peace. His ultimate highlight is not what he has been able to accomplish on the business front, but that he has been happily married to his university sweetheart, fathered three incredible kids and is now a grandfather.

'That we have remained happy in each other's company all these years is my crowning joy.'

ACCENTURE

# VUKANI MNGXATI

*The inclusivity enthusiast*

'I don't want to be the one making all the decisions.
When you have a broad team of fellow decision-makers, the chance of making
the right decisions is much higher and you minimise errors.'

As the CEO of professional services company Accenture South Africa, Vukani Mngxati moves in the upper echelons of society – but he still describes himself as a village boy.

Vukani was born in the hamlet of Highflats in rural KwaZulu-Natal in 1977 and wrote his matric exams at Bhekameva High School in Ixopo in 1995. The following year, he enrolled at what is today the University of KwaZulu-Natal for a Bachelor of Commerce in Information Technology and graduated in 1998.

In 2000, Vukani started at Accenture, a global Irish-American company that offers services in strategy and consulting, technology and operations. When the company flew him from Durban to his new station in Johannesburg, it was his first time on an aeroplane. The young man from the Zulu Kingdom was placed into an orientation programme for analysts and was fascinated by the country's commercial capital. Fascination turned to awe when he was inducted into a one-month programme in the US aimed at growing the technological capabilities of new recruits.

On his return, Vukani was deployed to the Independent Electoral Commission, where he worked for six years. A memorable accomplishment was taking part in building the results system of the commission, which was used in the local government elections of 2003. The system is still in use today.

After about seven years at Accenture, an exciting opportunity presented itself. Mondli Mlangeni, a close friend from his varsity days who had also worked at the company previously, had recently started his own consultancy called Nkunzini Consulting. He bid for and was awarded a consulting assignment in Durban.

'Mondli asked me to join him. I felt I knew enough at that stage to become his business partner,' Vukani recalls. 'I resigned from Accenture in 2007 and went back to KwaZulu-Natal to work with him. We signed up a few clients and employed about 40 members of staff.'

Within months, the company experienced rapid growth. 'All was going well, but then the global financial crisis hit ... we were forced to gracefully exit all our projects.'

Mlangeni and Vukani went into debt because they had to borrow money to pay out termination benefits for their employees. Today he refers to his three-year stint at Nkunzini as his 'Master of Business Administration degree' because of the valuable lessons learnt, which, he says, still apply today in his role at the top.

'A small company does not have the luxury of predictable cash flow; you must rely on every dollar made. At times you are literally living from hand to mouth, and you have to manage your earnings carefully. The demands on a business are significant and even basic things like rent and salaries can put pressure on cash. You must be very meticulous to keep the business profitable.'

Another key lesson was that management does not always have all the answers. In his career, Vukani has found that business solutions most often come from those working below him. He recalls multiple occasions when they were stuck and one of their consultants came up with a genius suggestion. Having the humility and the latitude to understand that others may know exactly how to address an issue can contribute greatly to a leader's success.

The third lesson from his Nkunzini experience is the importance of ethical business practice. With their government clients, there were occasions when those in charge would solicit under-the-table payments

ACCENTURE's **Vukani Mngxati**
*(Photo: Courtesy of Accenture)*

to sign off on projects. Vukani says they decided to walk away from any such deals, and he believes that he wouldn't be where he is today if he had given in.

When he resigned from Accenture the first time, the company said that 'they would always have space for him' should he want to return. Broke and jobless, Vukani made a call in 2010 to ask if the offer still stood. To his delight, Accenture welcomed their prodigal son back with open arms; they did not even subject him to a second interview process.

He was placed in the public sector division and quickly rose through the ranks. He was angling to take over the position of the head of the division when the incumbent, Livingstone Chilwane, moved on.

But then, in December 2017, he got a phone call from then CEO William Mzimba, summoning him to his office. He was asked to run the development of the local Accenture growth strategy.

Vukani ran strategy sessions with the entire firm in early 2018, and they were very well received. William decided to put both Livingstone and Vukani up as candidates to take over his job as managing director of Accenture South Africa. Vukani emerged as the successful candidate, taking over the reins in May 2018.

### A strategy through five lenses

Vukani says that when he took over, some employees were disillusioned, thinking that he would remove them from their jobs. 'Because of the transformation agenda, there were senior leaders who thought I was out to replace them with individuals from previously disadvantaged backgrounds. I had to help them understand that while we needed the leadership to reflect the country's demographics, we would be thoughtful about the process as a key priority was to drive business growth.'

Another issue Vukani encountered was that the executive leadership was not working as a unit. Everyone appeared to be pulling in a different direction, something he was not aware of before he assumed the position. Part of the reason was that there wasn't an effective strategy. Although Vukani had helped crafting the strategy earlier, he realised it was very theoretical.

'Comparing what we had documented in a book with what we were meant to execute in practice showed that our strategy was pie-in-the-sky kind of stuff,' Vukani says. 'We needed something simple that everybody could understand and would be able to articulate.'

So he decided to frame the strategy in terms of five lenses. The first was establishing a clarity of purpose – meant 'to create an abundance in Africa through technology and human ingenuity'.

The second lens was to identify their focus. Globally, the group had clients in 19 different industries, but not all of them were appropriate targets in the South African context. The strategy outlined ten industries they intended to develop strategic relationships with.

The third lens was identifying their clients. Not all companies within a particular industry were a good fit; they had to identify those that would make it worthwhile investing the time, capacity and thought leadership into.

The fourth lens was determining what they were going to sell. Accenture offers a plethora of services and not all of them would be applicable to the industries they aimed to serve in South Africa. They had to focus on a limited number of services to provide clarity both internally and to the market.

'We had to ask ourselves what the strategic growth priorities would be in those services,' Vukani continues. 'This is part of why we focused on cloud services and the customer agenda. It is also the reason for our acquisition of the King James Creative Agency, which helps us focus on putting creativity at the centre of experience-led transformation.'

The fifth lens was to identify talent. 'We needed to hire and develop the right people, who would be able to execute what we wanted to do for our clients,' Vukani explains.

Creating an effective strategy proved to be crucial during the COVID-19 pandemic when companies had to weather the slowdown in business activity. Because of the pandemic, Accenture lost several important clients, yet thanks to the strategy, the business is now seeing close to 30% top-line growth per annum.

'Our strategy helped us to create clarity for our people and the market about where we're headed. Everyone understands what is going on. Our people are able to distinguish between who we want to work for and who we do not necessarily want to prioritise. This is important, because without a guideline, they would not focus their attention where it matters most.'

### Inclusive leadership

For Vukani, the biggest win since taking up the top job is that his executive team now works as one. They've managed to change the culture of people being unsure of who their allies were, to such an extent that the team's members now feel that they're working towards a common future together.

Vukani advocates inclusive leadership. 'I don't want to be the one making all the decisions. When you have a broad team of fellow decision-makers, the chance of making the right decision is much higher and you minimise errors. Even when you do make mistakes, you can work together to reverse the effects. I do not believe one can be right all the time, so I always look to give other brains an opportunity to contribute.'

It's easy to make a decision when you must choose between what is right and what is wrong, says Vukani. It becomes much more difficult to make a call when both decisions are potentially right. 'For example, when selecting someone for promotion, you can decide to prioritise diversity or you can decide to prioritise skills. Both are noble priorities and present a dilemma. A good leader is decisive; they make calls even if it is a difficult one because it is no use sitting on the fence.'

Vukani believes good leaders also show kindness and empathy. Humans are emotional beings and connecting with them and demonstrating that you genuinely care for their well-being can be very powerful.

'I'm a mental health advocate,' Vukani reveals. 'I see a therapist every second week. Some people might think it's a sign of weakness, but it's actually a sign of strength because no one can pour from an empty cup. Being a CEO of an organisation like this can be tough. So, ensuring that you're in the correct mental state and having help to deal with stress allow you to be successful.'

Outside the office, Vukani enjoys keeping fit. He spends a lot of time at the gym, which gives him time to think. He also runs and cycles on weekends, allowing him to breathe deeply and connect with fellow outdoor enthusiasts.

# EMRIE BROWN

*A pioneering woman in banking*

'An organisation is like an orchestra, if the participants
are not in sync, they can learn all the notes and play but the
performance will not give the audience goosebumps.'

When Emrie Brown, the youngest of four children, walked out of university with a cum laude degree in accounting, she could not have made her parents more proud. Her father was a fitter and turner at the national railways and her mother was a bookkeeper, and with a big family to support, there wasn't money for Emrie's studies.

So she sought a scholarship to fund her studies at the University of Pretoria (UP) and graduated top of her class in 1990. A year later she completed her honours degree at the then Rand Afrikaans University (today University of Johannesburg), with results just as good. She subsequently joined KPMG in Pretoria for articles and – in true Emrie style – was ranked second in the 1992 SA Institute of Chartered Accountants board examinations. But she quickly realised she was not cut out to be an auditor, and left KPMG as soon as the three-year contract was complete.

As a newly minted chartered accountant, she took up a position as junior lecturer at UP while deciding what career path she wanted to take. She chose investment banking and she applied to several financial institutions, receiving offers from two of them. She settled on Nedbank because most of the staff spoke Afrikaans, a language she felt more comfortable in at the time. Emrie was the first female transactor at Nedbank Investment Bank, and by the time she left to join

RMB's **Emrie Brown**
*(Photo: Cathy Pinnock, Yip Photography)*

Rand Merchant Bank (RMB), not much had changed in the banking world.

In 2006, after five years as an investment banker at RMB, Emrie was promoted to head up the leveraged finance unit – the first time a woman was responsible for a profit centre at the bank. In 2009, she left the bank and moved to Cape Town, as she became a mother to the first of her two boys at age 41 (the second arrived two years later).

Curious, I ask her how it worked for her to have children in her forties.

'It worked well for me!' she laughs. 'I guess I was so engrossed in my career in my thirties and focused on achieving so much growth that I didn't have time to start a family. Actually, I thought that career success and motherhood were mutually exclusive, but looking back, I know that's not the case. I advise women to make a conscious decision about children and to not leave it until it is too late. Choosing not to have children is also perfectly fine, because parenting is not for everyone.'

Emrie has found that motherhood is not an impediment to career progression because women have all the necessary leadership traits to make a success of managing others. All it takes is to believe in yourself and to understand that you're well equipped to lead. Women should take confidence from knowing that they bring a different voice to organisations and 'they should wear their female badge with pride', she says.

Emrie writes on the RMB website that 'your career can be much more like a jungle gym than the traditional career ladder in your journey to achieve success,' paraphrasing Sheryl Sandberg, author of *Lean In: Women, Work, and the Will to Lead*. 'How you define success and the sacrifices that you are prepared to make, are decisions that will be required along the way and will be different for each person. As women we don't have to "man up" to be successful in financial services,' she continues.

## *Many firsts at RMB*

Emrie missed RMB too much and stayed away for only six months. She was promoted to head of the investment bank in 2015 and head of the banking division in 2019. In October 2022, she took over as the first female CEO of RMB Corporate and Investment Bank.

I ask her what it means to her to be a woman of many firsts in the banking world.

'In the moment, I didn't appreciate the significance of it,' she answers. 'In investment banking, it is your intellectual and interpersonal skills that get you ahead rather than physical power, so on paper it should be easy for women to compete on an equal footing. It dawned on me only later how significant my appointments were for women in banking. Our research shows that women generally do not move to the next layer of management in the financial services industry – not only locally, but worldwide.

'I think this places a big responsibility on me and other women in leadership positions to pave the way for young women to rise through the ranks. When I got into investment banking in 1997, it was a lot harder to find women in these spaces and much harder to have your voice heard. Diversity is a great thing for businesses because they can benefit from varied perspectives, but minorities in any grouping struggle to express their views because they may appear so different from the norm.

'We are making progress on the diversification front by having more women in client-facing roles, unlike in the past when women were relegated to support functions. But it's not yet enough. Men still dominate leadership positions and there is an unconscious bias when it comes to promotions. People tend to think that only someone who is a lot like them is capable of filling their shoes.'

The highlight of Emrie's career is the change she is seeing at RMB. The face of the organisation has changed significantly over the years, with more women and previously disadvantaged demographics occupying leadership positions. When she was appointed to the RMB executive committee there were only two women at that level. Today that number has doubled and there are at least two women heading profit-generating businesses.

The two most significant lows in her career were dealing with the global financial crisis and the COVID-19 pandemic. These were curveballs for the financial services industry as borrowers struggled to honour their instalments. For Emrie, the key was not to panic and to believe that they could get through these crises without dropping their clients. 'It would have been easy to end relationships and to tell clients "we will be back when things improve". That would go against our values, as we believe in supporting our customers through difficult times and to foster a common mindset.'

### Success X factors

Some of the leadership lessons that Emrie picked up from tough times include having the right team 'on the bus' – you are only as strong as your weakest link, she says. The best team is one that shares the vision of the organisation and embraces excellence. Excellence does not mean perfection; rather, it is expected that mistakes will be made along the way but the key is to ensure you learn from them. The right team comprises people who are passionate about what they do and do not come to work just to earn a salary.

Emrie advises professionals to find a career where they have a passion for their work and the mission of the organisation. This, she says, is where you will find that you don't mind to go the extra mile and you never struggle to bring the best version of yourself. An organisation of people who are energised by their work has an incredible impact and employees should not shy away from changing jobs if they find that they're not enjoying it.

'This was my experience during my six months away from RMB,' recalls Emrie. 'I briefly joined another financial institution, but quickly felt that the culture was not for me. All banks in South Africa are somewhat successful but they are incredibly different. To quote [management consultant] Peter Drucker, "culture eats strategy for breakfast" and I simply could not resonate with the culture there. An organisation is like an orchestra: if the participants are not in sync, they can learn all the notes and play but the performance will not give the audience goosebumps.

'The right culture creates an environment that pulls people together and unites them around a common vision to outperform their peers. It is one that encourages work–life integration as opposed to work–life balance, which is something I firmly believe in. I really love my job and look at how I can integrate my life into it. I want to be the best for my job and the best for my family. It is an aspiration to give each the best and not to neglect either.'

### Plans as CEO

'I believe that we've created an empowering culture at RMB, one where we have enabled dealmakers to structure solutions for clients. We give them the responsibility to grow the organisation by charging them with the entire spectrum of client engagement, end to end. We have a non-hierarchical structure where the most junior person can set up a meeting with me, whereas in other organisations, you have to send an email to your immediate superior who then sends the message up the chain and waits for a response to come back down again. We see ourselves as an organisation of care where we are the trusted advisors to design unique solutions for clients.'

'So what lies ahead?' I ask.

Emrie stresses that the value of care involves having concern for each other within the organisation and for clients. In taking over the CEO role from James Formby, she became only the second woman to lead a corporate and investment banking unit in South Africa, alongside Nedbank's Anel Bosman. She will serve for a seven-year stint at RMB, which is the normative term for a CEO at the organisation.

Emrie plans to continue leading her teams to awards as she did as the head of the banking division. Under her leadership, the division won 'The Banker' award for the most innovative investment bank in Africa four years in a row (from 2016 to 2019), the M&A Today Global 100 Investment Bank of the Year in Africa in 2020, the Global Finance Best Bank in Africa for New Financial Technology, the Spire Best Debt Origination Team on the JSE for 10 consecutive years from 2010 to 2019 and the Dealmaker's Best BEE Investment Adviser in 2019.

'I have big things to focus on as CEO,' says Emrie. 'The first is to look after our people. International banks are looking to take our top talent and for professionals under 35, it is an attractive prospect to go and work in a developed market and to earn hard currency. We will have to focus a lot on attracting and retaining talent. The financial services industry is changing rapidly and we need to invest in technology to remain efficient. We need to make sure that our business evolves to keep on delivering digital offerings to our clients.

'I'm invested in South Africa and I think corporate citizens have a big role in improving our current situation and to ensure we have future success. I have never contemplated emigrating and I never will. People think the rest of the world is a lot better, but it really isn't. Just look at the economic challenges in the UK, for example. Of course, things like loadshedding are unwelcome, because companies have to invest in backup power, which impacts employment. But the solution is not to leave. I believe we can work through our problems together.'

Emrie freely shares her life story with her colleagues to help them understand that what she has achieved is a result of working hard and seizing opportunities. She says she always tries to bring humour to her management style and to see things positively. The glass is always half full in her eyes. 'Investment banking can be a highly stressful environment and my view is that we should take the work that we do seriously but not take ourselves seriously.'

Proof that Emrie is fun loving is her affinity for fast cars. She is a self-confessed petrol junkie who swaps the family Land Rover Defender for a Porsche 911 Targa on weekends. Nothing excites her more than putting her foot down and hearing the engine roar as the machine motors down an open highway.

# NOTES

1   Clarke, Peter. *A Question of Leadership: From Gladstone to Thatcher*, London: Penguin, 1992

2   Caro, Robert. *Working: Researching, Interviewing, Writing*. New York: Knopf, 2019.

3   Vodacom Group, annual financial statements, 2022

4   Capitec Bank, annual financial statements, 2022

5   Motus Group, annual financial statements, 2022

6   *Financial Mail*, 30 July 2020, https://www.businesslive.co.za/fm/features/cover-story/2020-07-30-christo-wiese-how-do-you-recover-from-losing-r125bn/

7   Curro Annual Integrated Report, 2021

8   Stadio Interim Financial Results, 30 June 2022

9   Clarke, Peter. *A Question of Leadership: From Gladstone to Thatcher*, London: Penguin, 1992

# ACKNOWLEDGEMENTS

This work would not be possible without the support of my dear wife Mueni.

To Sue Nyathi, thank you for introducing me to the world of the published.

Annie Olivier, you're a dream publisher. Thank you for working with me – it's now two books and counting!

Finally, my sincere gratitude to all those who helped me connect with the voices captured in this book: Roy Mutooni, Chio Sakutukwa, Lindi Mbugua, Nick Ndiritu, Deon Viljoen, Stephen Chege, Glenn Fullerton, Mike Davis, Rose Mamabolo, Phakamisa Ndzamela and Grathel Motau.

# ABOUT THE AUTHOR

**KC ROTTOK CHESAINA** is a chartered accountant with a master's degree in commerce. He is a former partner in the international audit firm RSM and founder of *The African Professional Magazine* and the SA Professional Services Awards.

A fellow of the Bloomberg Media Initiative, Chesaina currently serves as a financial reporting adviser at W.consulting.

His first book *Masters of Money: Strategies for Success from the CFOs of South Africa's Biggest Companies* was published in 2022.

**KC  Rottok Chesaina**
*(Photo: Mzu Nhlabati)*